WHAT PEOPLE ARE SAYING ...

"I have practiced condominium law in this part of the country for fifteen years. Leo's stories seem unbelievable, but I can attest that they are true. He does a great job of describing the outrageous ways that people behave and misbehave when living in a condominium community."

~ Aaron Marines, Esquire

"Leo always tells the truth, and he tells it with wit, empathy, and a great deal of humor. His commentary about the future of the condo concept should be read carefully. No one understands the condominium lifestyle better than Leo Rosenberger."

~ E. Ray Young, HOA Board President

"No one knows condos like Leo Rosenberger. From rabid cats to tangled squirrels and through all the demands, antics, and foibles of condo residents, Leo is the gold standard."

~ Del Staecker, Award-Winning Author

D1593745

CONDO MANIA

An Entertaining Guide for Condo Owners, Board Members, and Homeowners Association Managers

by

To Ryan...

Truth is Power!

LEO ROSENBERGER

Leo Rosenberger

Red Engine Press
Pittsburgh, PA

978-1-943267-09-5 - Trade Paperback

Red Engine Press
Pittsburgh, PA
Printed in the United States.

This book is dedicated to my parents
Leo Sr. and Rita,
my daughters Leigh and Ruthie,
and their mom Pamela
who was equally responsible
for their well-being and success.

Newlyweds Leo Sr. and Rita, 1938

Two roads diverged in a wood, and I—
I took the one less traveled by,
And that has made all the difference.
~Robert Frost
The Road Not Taken

CONTENTS

What Does the Budget Mean for Association Owners?

Be a Good Board Member
Work with Difficult Personalities
Stay Out of Debt
Respect Your Elders
Live a Full Life

ACKNOWLEDGMENTS

This book would not have been possible without the upbringing my dad and mom provided. If they were alive today, they would see that I ended up living an independent life that would have met with their approval.

Furthermore, I passed their lessons on to my two daughters Leigh and Ruthie, who both graduated from the United States Military Academy at West Point, New York, and are currently serving as officers in the United States Army.

I would also like to thank my administrative assistant of twenty years, Ann Oswald, who shared and endured most of my condo experiences.

Leigh Sherrard Rosenberger,
West Point 2012

Ruth Ellyn Rosenberger,
West Point 2014

PREFACE

Like many country boys born in 1949, I was raised to be self-sufficient in all aspects of life. Being the fourth of five children, I received the benefits not only of my parents' lessons, but also those of my elder siblings. There was no lack of advice in the Rosenberger household.

My dad was a farm boy from the dairy farm region of the southern Catskill Mountains in New York. He left the farm in his late teens to live with a sister (one of seven siblings) in New York City. He always said that if he hadn't left the farm, his father would have worked him to death. He met my mom in the city, suffered through the Great Depression, had a crippling leg accident, and eventually moved back to the country about four miles from his boyhood farm homestead. There, in Hortonville, New York, he built and established Leo's Market, a country general store, delicatessen, and Mobil gas station.

Leo Sr. was the type of man who wanted his children to know everything that he had learned in his life. He was a hands-on educator with a lot of patience.

All of the Rosenberger children helped mind the store from the time they entered grade school until they graduated from high school and headed for college. While we were in school, my mom ran the store and gas station by herself since my dad worked for the county highway department, driving heavy trucks for road construction and snow plowing.

Leo Sr. was the type of man who wanted his children to know everything that he had learned in his life. He was a hands-on educator with a lot of patience. He had to have his sons right next to him, learning how to handle money and give change, converse with customers, and build and repair stuff. In our spare time, he taught us how to hunt, fish, and trap. He showed us how to tap the maple trees to gather sap to make maple syrup. We gathered apples from my aunt's farm and took them to the local cider mill, selling the cider in our store. Dad helped us establish a small business of catching live bait, minnows, and night crawlers, and selling them to the tourist fishermen.

My dad believed that the more self-sufficient a man could be, the less he had to rely on others for his health and welfare. His lessons were always about working hard (not wasting time), staying strong and healthy, and reading as much as possible. This was my dad's legacy. He didn't want his children to be beholden to anyone. And above all, we were expected to be truthful and treat others as we would like to be treated.

Being the fourth of five children meant that I worked my way through college, since my older siblings all received some college financing ahead of me. My work-and-pay-as-you-go college attendance plan continued to add to my long list of various employments that provided a wealth of education and experience beyond what is represented by any college degree. Most of my peers simply got a college degree and went to work in their particular field. I took the "road less traveled" and ended up gaining invaluable knowledge and insight into many different areas. Although I experienced uncertainty about where I would end up, I had a good sense of conviction that I was going in the right direction. My instinctive nature and upbringing gave me the tools and self-confidence to confront life's challenges on my own terms.

In chronological order from 1957, I was a newspaper boy, gas station attendant, soda jerk, dairy farmhand, beer truck helper, lifeguard, railroad trackman, racetrack usher, mailman, sawmill laborer, supermarket clerk, mental facility orderly, United States Army soldier, sporting goods salesman, masonry laborer, bricklayer, fitness instructor, pizza maker, drill press operator, stainless steel polisher, carpet cleaner, waiter, house painter, trucking company dock worker, forklift operator, CPA firm staff accountant, corporate accountant: tax return preparation, independent CPA, charity fundraiser, stock broker, vice president of financial services, college financial counselor, community association manager/treasurer/consultant, and author.

Leo's Market, 1943

INTRODUCTION

I did not plan to spend one-third of my life-to-date in the condominium association management industry. It just happened. Fortunately, having an unexpected situation and eventual profession dumped in one's lap couldn't have happened to a better person—me.

It all started in the autumn of 1989, when I was approached by a group of owners who were unhappy with the mismanagement of several issues in the community.

It all began when my elderly parents, who were living in a rural area of New York's Catskill Mountains, began to experience the trials and tribulations of old age. Being somewhat of a visionary, I began hinting to my parents about moving to an area that could better accommodate elderly living needs. For the most part, those hints and suggestions fell upon deaf ears until the day that I got "the call." That call from my parents would necessitate a quick move to a more suburban setting with elderly long-term care services. Where? The area of my residence in Lancaster County, Pennsylvania.

Although I was the fourth of five children, the circumstances of geography, gender, age, and family status dictated that I was the one who would have the main responsibility for my parents' health and welfare. That was okay with my siblings and me, as we all loved them and were grateful for all the sacrifices they had made for us on our way to maturity and independence.

While my wife Pamela searched furiously for a new residence for my parents, I visited them in New York to tell them they were moving to Lancaster, Pennsylvania. This announcement did not go over well with my mom, who had envisioned spending her remaining years with her oldest daughter in New Jersey. Dad was a bit more open-minded about the move.

Pam was quick to zero in on an easily accessible, two bedroom condo unit about four miles from our residence. I had lived in this community when it was a newly constructed apartment complex named Glencreek Apartments. It was a singles community in the 70s that had eventually been converted from rentals to private ownership condos in 1982. We purchased a unit in 1986 and rented it to my parents.

The relocation of my parents from New York to Pennsylvania was accomplished by my brother and me in a twenty-four-hour moving marathon. My parents adjusted rapidly to their new surroundings with the help of my siblings during the early months of their new residency. Their immediate worries and problems were solved. It would only be three short years until mine would begin.

It all started in the autumn of 1989, when I was approached by a group of Glencreek activists who were unhappy with the mismanagement of several issues in the community. I was unaware of any problems, as I had been devoting all of my attention to the birth of my first child, a daughter named Leigh. I am not sure how or why I was designated to be the star recruit of this activist group. Perhaps it was because I was an energetic forty-year-old with a CPA license and construction experience. They approached me to help them with their plans to reject the proposed 1990-1991 budget and remove the entire board of directors from the community's governance.

The current executive board members' only qualifications were that they were somewhat successful businessmen.

In other words, they thought that if they were successful in their businesses, they would be successful at condo management. Not! In reality, just because a board member's private business sells millions of widgets, it doesn't assure that he will be an honest, efficient, and successful condominium association board director. Some of the board members owned multiple units and, as a result, had become very self-serving. Other board members just followed suit out of disinterest or ignorance of condo law.

At the time, I was a new retail financial consultant for Shearson Lehman Brothers, a major Wall Street firm. But I made time to educate myself on condo management. For about six months during the fall of 1989 and winter of 1990, I stopped in at Glencreek's community management office on my way to work. During these office visits, I read all the board meeting minutes from May 1982 through March of 1990. I also reviewed construction contracts, service contracts, and insurance policies, all the while taking notes. This self-imposed condo crash course was informative, to say the least. It was also shocking.

One board sympathizer exclaimed, "Who the hell is this guy and where did he come from?"

Prior to that autumn of 1989, I knew little about Pennsylvania condominium law and management. I just paid my monthly assessment like everyone else. However, what I did know was that I had a solid code of ethics, an abundance of country common sense, and knowledge of business law. From what I discovered in my six-month review of Glencreek's governance, all three were severely lacking. What could I do?

Somehow I obtained a two-inch-thick book entitled *Pennsylvania Condominium Law and Practice*. I marked up the sections that were applicable to the questionable practices I had discovered in my review of Glencreek's records. Then, armed with my CPA knowledge, a limited understanding of condo law, and my tenacious spirit, I attended a pre-election open meeting of the association.

Most of the disgruntled attendees (this was the largest open meeting attendance in the history of the association) did not know me. The crowd was standing room only and borderline riotous. During my interrogation of board members and officers, the meeting tension escalated. One board sympathizer exclaimed to the audience, "Who the hell is this guy and where did he come from?"

The majority of unit owners in attendance came to my defense, allowing me to resume my exposé of the sins of the Glencreek Association "Fathers." And there were many—so many that I only concentrated on the most egregious. I knew that would be enough to enable a "changing of the guard."

At the election the following month, I was voted into office, along with two others. All three of the current board members whose term was ending lost their bids for reelection. In the next few months, two more board members quit and one died. This gave the Glencreek condominium community a chance to start fresh.

Board membership was my introduction to the condo industry and lifestyle, and it was a "baptism by fire." I stayed on as a board member for fourteen years until I retired from my profession as a vice-president of sales for Citigroup Smith Barney. After a two year hiatus, during which I was still a part of the Glencreek executive board, I established myself in a post-retirement career as a community association manager, specializing in condo associations. Only then did I really come to understand the intricacies of all aspects of the condominium lifestyle.

Since 1982, time and experience has proven that successful condo community management requires a unique skill set that has yet to be formulated into a formal, educational program as of the date of this writing. Consequently, there are not very many well-managed condominium associations. [See Appendix A for my suggested curriculum of prospective courses for an associate degree in community association management.]

I am an anomaly in the current world of condo association management. Though being a past member of Community Association Institute (CAI) with a couple of management certifications has helped me, it was not the key to my management success. My management success came from the following:

- [ ] CPA license
- [ ] Construction experience
- [ ] Public speaking ability
- [ ] A "thick skin"
- [ ] Maturity (becoming a manager at the age of fifty-four)
- [ ] Condominium board tenure of fourteen years before becoming a manager

Another feature of my success as a manager is that I do not use email in any aspect of the business. As a matter of fact, I seldom have to write a letter to solve a problem. For the most part, my problems are solved face to face or by a phone conversation. My communication style was formulated and instilled in me many years ago by caring parents, older siblings, and Catholic nuns. My siblings and I were taught to write inspirationally, speak clearly, and conduct ourselves in a respectable and reasonable manner. I was taught to treat others as I would like to be treated. Emailing and texting do nothing to enhance my time-tested skill set. Those electronic aids would never enable me to manage properties as well as I can manage (four) by doing it in my own hands-on way.

By comparison, many property management companies fill their management positions with individuals who have to spend an enormous amount of their valuable time answering emails from the loudest complainers. This is not an effective long-term management strategy. What is the turnover rate for such community managers? High enough to be a contributing factor in how I acquired my community association clients: the property management companies exhausted their supply of managers (and the patience of their soon-to-be former clients).

In the pages that follow, I offer my insights into condominium living and management as well as the insights of a sixty-six-year-old who has been involved with the condo concept for almost thirty years. I will cover all aspects of homeowner association management through the use of technical instruction, street-smart experience, and real-life stories ranging from the ridiculous to the sublime.

Throughout this book you will see me frequently use the words "common sense." After reading this book, I think you will agree that when it comes to condos, I have "been there, done that." Hopefully the book will have a positive impact on your condo experience.

Leo receiving Gold Star Awards for the communities he managed.

Chapter 1

CAREFREE LIVING
TRUE OR FALSE?

Condo Nuances

What is a condominium? It is a form of property ownership. The word's origin is from two Latin words: "con," meaning joint, and "dominium," meaning rule or sovereignty. Hence, "joint rule" or "joint control." In real estate terminology, it is the individual ownership of a unit in a multi-unit structure.

Condominium associations contain two distinct types of property: individual building units and common elements. In a condominium, an individual owns a unit and an undivided interest in the common elements of the entire community or building. The individual units are the residences set aside for ownership and occupancy. The common elements are, generally speaking, everything outside the boundaries of the individual units. They constitute portions of the structure that support, endorse, or service the units (bearing walls, roofs, gutters and downspouts, plumbing, etc.). Common elements also include amenities such as private roads, parking areas, landscaping, sidewalks, maintenance buildings, clubhouses, swimming pools, and athletic facilities.

Each owner of a residential unit owns an individual interest in the common elements. This individual interest is a fractional share of ownership called a "percentage interest" and includes everything outside the living unit's internal boundaries, as defined in the condominium declaration. It is this interest that gives individual association members the right to participate in the use of the common elements. It also gives the unit owner the right to one vote in the association's board member elections.

Condo ownership obligates each owner (association member) to pay a share of the expenses for maintaining and replacing the community's facilities and landscape. These shares of the common expenses are referred to as association dues, and are collected from the individual owners on a monthly, quarterly, or annual basis, depending on the association bylaws and declaration.

Additionally, each unit owner is taxed separately for real estate and school taxes; the association pays neither of these taxes. Although the condo association completes an annual tax return, it owns no property and consequently pays no real estate taxes. No unit owner is liable for the taxes of any other unit. Also, no unit owner is subject to the lien of a mortgage on any other unit in the association

Why Buy a Condo?

Well, there could be one big reason or a variety of reasons. As someone who has experienced every aspect of condo life from every possible perspective over the past thirty years, here are my observations.

For many people it is a financial decision to buy into a condo community as a resident. It may be as simple as, "It's all I can afford." Or it might be a question of convenience— no outside building or landscape maintenance. The amenities offered by condo communities, such as pools, clubhouses, and other recreational facilities or functions, may be a big draw for some condo buyers. It could be location—closer to shopping or elder care service providers. For the older population, it could be a retirement lifestyle that is less expensive than detached home ownership. Many people over fifty years of age prefer to live among peers of similar age or lifestyle requirements. Sidewalks and building designs that accommodate an older or physically handicapped demographic could be a big selling point.

If one, some, or all of the above considerations caused you to buy into the condo concept of living, then you also subjected yourself to a lifestyle that needs to be controlled for it to happen in the first place. Without efficient, responsible, and reliable management controls, condo living can be miserable for all. In order to have the type of condo community that most people desire (a high quality lifestyle at the lowest cost), there needs to be compliance to the condo association's declaration, bylaws, and community policies and procedures. Accomplishing this compliance is the responsibility of the board of directors through its management and maintenance personnel. However, no matter how hard they try to uphold community standards—there will always be those owners for whom condo living was probably not the right choice.

Ten Reasons Condo Living Might Not Be for You

1. You want to display the best ceramic lawn ornament collection in the country.
2. When the grass is cut in front of your unit, you don't like that it leans different ways.
3. Feral cats wait in line to eat dinner at your unit.
4. Your unit is always the one to be shoveled out last after a snowstorm.
5. Your handicap space is too small for your school bus.
6. You believe that the best time to complain to management is at the association parties.
7. You believe that they are your flowers, trees and shrubs, but the weeding belongs to the association.

8. After you move in, you learn that there is a monthly maintenance fee.

9. Your friends have to pay to go in the pool.

10. You feel that people who do not vote at annual board elections should be counted as "no" votes, except when you run for the board.

If . . . The Biggest Word in Condo Living

As a community association manager and consultant, I have to consider the word "if" a lot. For example:

If one resident from every unit came to the pool on the same afternoon, the pool would be too crowded. That is why the pool policy has to limit the number of passes each unit owner receives. Units with multiple owners and large families who do not live in the community require some type of restricted attendance. The pool is not that big.

If pool goers closed their table umbrellas before they left the pool area, it would be one less chore for the manager.

If every unit were allowed to have five garden ornaments, the landscaping would look a little too busy. Do we really want that many gazing balls? When you gaze at the ball don't you just see your own face?

If residents would slow down, we wouldn't need speed bumps.

If residents didn't feed stray cats, there wouldn't be a feral feline problem.

If residents read their resident's manual, they would see that it addresses the aforementioned issues and many others.

My dad used to say that "If the pilgrims would have shot a skunk, Thanksgiving would be different." Well, if residents don't comply with community standards, won't the community be different? Will it be better or worse? The message here is that if the manager allows one resident's eccentricity, he should allow another's. Where does the eccentricity end? It probably ends in a really goofy looking community.

Where Do We Go From Here?

Condominium communities or high rise condos were planned, built, and marketed as the ideal lifestyle for those who were looking for fewer maintenance responsibilities and the benefits of amenities they couldn't afford on their own. They were intended to be homogenized communities of people of similar age and lifestyle who wanted carefree living, free of maintenance and security responsibilities.

But before the nuances of the condo lifestyle can be fully appreciated, a brief history of the condominium concept of living is required.

Chapter 2

DOES HISTORY
REPEAT ITSELF?

The Utopian Concept

The perception of condominiums in the United States is that they are a relatively modern concept beginning in the 1950s. The first condos appeared in the United States in the territory of Puerto Rico in 1958, but the concept of condo living can be traced back hundreds of years. Some extreme research has found hints of condo type living as far back as the sixth century B.C. In the 1500s and 1600s, what we today call condo communities would have been called intentional communities or utopias. People of like-mindedness came together to form communities that possessed highly desirable, near perfect, qualities.

The word "utopia" comes from two Greek words, "ou" and "topos," meaning "no" and "place," hence, "no place." It was meant to be a place of ideal perfection, especially regarding laws, government, and social conditions—a place one could only dream about. Ever since Sir Thomas More presented his 1516 book entitled *Utopia*, describing a fictional island society in the Atlantic Ocean, many attempts have been made to establish homogenized, condo-like communities. Some examples are the Ephrata Cloisters in Pennsylvania; the Shakers; and one of my era's favorites, Wavy Gravy's "Hog Farm" in 1966 in Llano, New Mexico. As an admitted "tech-luddite," I would have felt at home in the Green Bank Community of West Virginia, where Wi-Fi and cell phones were banned. This community was safe from the reach of technology, a place where electro-sensitive people could escape the digital world. All of these communities thought they held the keys to a wonderful life, but proved themselves to be impractical schemes for social improvement.

How can so many people with different perspectives on life live together in a condensed condo community?

Were today's condo communities intended to be such paradises when established? Like their predecessor utopian communities, modern condo communities should consist of individuals who share a common vision of the experiences that make up a happy life. However, with the ever-increasing diversity of American culture in major urban areas, it's difficult to garner the homogeneity necessary to maintain a successful condo community. How can boards and managers establish policies and enforce rules in a community made up of different nationalities, races, religions, sexual and gender preferences, ages, and economic backgrounds?

How can so many people with different perspectives on life live together in a condensed condo community? In Ottawa, Canada, a family was evicted from a rented condo after neighbors complained of noise from an indoor trampoline being used by an autistic son. And how about the woman who moved into a high-rise condo, removed the wall-to-wall carpeting, and installed a hardwood floor for her new dance studio? Lawsuits ensued in both instances. How would you like to be a "mind-your-own-business" resident in one of those condos and end up paying a special assessment for lawyers to figure out the solution?

What has happened to this utopia-like condominium concept? Why the need for an in-depth explanation to potential buyers and managers of this lifestyle so suited for carefree living or one's retirement years? Since there will be about eighty million baby boomers retiring over the next fifteen years or so, the concept requires further understanding.

The Dilution Factor

In my opinion, the current condo model and its related governance problems are suffering due to the "dilution of homogenization" or as I call it, "DOH." The early condo demographics of the 50s, 60s, 70s, and 80s were the first retiree generations of America's modern industrialized society. These retirees were a relatively homogeneous group. They lived through the Great Depression, two world wars, the cold war, the civil rights movement, a presidential assassination, and men walking on the moon. They accomplished a lot together. There were deep common bonds.

Most of these early condo dwellers' lives were lived prior to the convenience and comfort of cheap airfare and air conditioning. I remember when the residents of major northeast cities escaped to the country (i.e., New Yorkers to the Catskills) to get away from the summer's sweltering heat for a few weeks. But what did they do when they retired and could live anywhere? Well, air conditioning killed the Catskills' resort industry and other similar getaway locations in the northeast. The South and Southwest United States became the beneficiaries of the retirees' lifestyle choices (the Carolinas, Florida, and Arizona). This homogeneous group, also known as the "Greatest Generation," thought alike in many ways. Their pre-retirement lives proved to them the benefits and rewards of working together for a common good. Simply put, they were more likely to get along together and be governed by one set of condo rules. If any demographic group could approach a utopian lifestyle through condo living, this post-World War II generation was it.

My thirty-year condo experience causes me to doubt that the current condo industry with its various state-by-state laws and management models is a viable solution to the carefree lifestyle envisioned by present and future retirees or, for that matter, anyone buying into the condo lifestyle for any reason.

The homogeneity of the aforementioned condo pioneers is becoming severely diluted. Those pioneers are either dead or are moving into long-term care communities or facilities. They are being replaced by upwardly mobile professionals who don't want the time, energy, and financial responsibilities of detached home ownership. Add to this group a younger generation of first-time home buyers whose budget is $200,000 or less since the real estate crash of 2008. All of a sudden we have a rapidly growing heterogeneous condo demographic in terms of age, finances, politics, nationality, and sexual preference. How can the boilerplate, one-size-fits-all, condo declarations and bylaws of the early condo years in the United States govern such a heterogeneous residential demographic?

Dystopian Tendencies

Present day condo communities are, in reality, utopian communities without the utopia. In fact, many of them could be called dystopias. Unless current and future condo association boards can hire gluttons for punishment who are willing to take on the herculean task of managing their communities, the future of peaceful and carefree living does not look as inviting as it did for Arizona's once-celebrated Sun City.

Somehow, within this context, I have successfully managed a few communities simultaneously over the years and consulted for several others on a fee per hour basis. I contend that, without a major overhaul of the condo industry from condo developers to condo boards and managers, the dreams of condo enthusiasts will become nightmares dominated by condo dispute resolution attorneys. There will be Condo Mania!

As I put the finishing touches on this book, I've had to deal with alcohol use in the baby pool (not underage drinking), a prison parolee desiring the condo lifestyle, and the shooting of rabid feral cats in a community. Stay tuned. Perhaps *Condo Mania Part II* will be a future necessity.

Changing Times

Condo living will likely be the preferred lifestyle of the baby boomers. Unlike previous generations, the boomers will seek a more active and managed lifestyle than their more sedentary predecessors. They are looking for more than just a house to live in.

Speaking about the Glencreek condos in my region of Pennsylvania, approximately 100 units have changed ownership in the last four years. The 70- to 90-year-olds are being replaced by 55- to 70-year-olds and younger. In Lancaster and Lebanon counties, various types of condo communities are being established. In fact, condo communities are being established all around us. In the last four years, condo communities with lifestyle amenities have appeared in East Hempfield, Mount Joy, Manheim, Lampeter, and Cornwall, to name a few. These new developments have more contemporary floor plans, garages, clubhouses, pools, tennis courts, and even golf courses.

How does a condominium association compete with this accelerating condo development and maintain its market appeal? Future association boards must focus on instituting (or maintaining and enhancing) the following:

- ☐ On-site management and maintenance staff with experience and good equipment
- ☐ Protection and enhancement of landscape, clubhouse, pool, and tennis courts
- ☐ Lifestyle enhancement with generation of good will through popular social and recreational events

- ☐ Competitive condo fees
- ☐ Generation of as much non-assessment income as possible from in-house maintenance, payment for pool guests, newsletter ads, interest income, collection of late fees, social events, and clubhouse rentals
- ☐ Capital reserve build-up
- ☐ Board interest and participation

The famous line, "the times they are a-changin'," from a Bob Dylan song of the same title, couldn't be more prophetic for the future of the condo lifestyle. We must pay attention to the present and not take past successes for granted. We must adapt to the changing demographics and try to accommodate as well as possible.

Chapter 3

WHO'S THE BOSS?

The "boss" of a homeowner association is its elected executive board (board of directors), led by the president of the board. The board is elected by vote of all the unit owners in the community, so in a sense, each homeowner is partially the boss. Collectively, homeowners "hire" the board and "fire" the board.

The word "resident" should not be interpreted as "unit owner" or "association member." Non owner residents are not members of the association.

Since the vast majority of HOA boards consist of unpaid volunteers who are inexperienced with an HOA's daily operation, they often delegate their authority as the "boss" to an off-site property management company or an in-house community association manager (such as myself). Only in the smallest communities do executive boards attempt to manage themselves. The failure rate for such attempts is very high.

Voting Members

Buying a condominium should not be considered lightly. The buyer should understand what condo living is all about and how the condominium association operates. Specific laws govern the operation of condo associations (and vary from state to state), but if the executive boards are not dedicated to the task or the association manager is not deeply involved in the day-to-day operations, laws may not offer much comfort to the unwary buyer. For instance, in Pennsylvania a condominium association consists of all the unit owners acting as a group in accordance with Pennsylvania Uniform Condominium Act, the association declaration, and the association bylaws. When one buys into a condominium community he subjects himself to living in a democracy governed by a declaration, bylaws, and resident's manual. Majority rule—a key ingredient of this democracy—may not be his or her cup of tea.

On a side note, non owner residents, including tenants and live-in guests, are not members of the association. There should be no circumstance in which the association should have to retain an attorney and incur legal expense to defend itself against non-association members who live in the community and feel their rights have been violated. The actions of a condominium association are not subject to the First Amendment. Pennsylvania common law is clear on this issue. A condominium association is a private actor and not a government entity. Threats of civil rights actions and First Amendment challenges by the non-member residents are particularly offensive and only serve to add fuel to minority issue embers. The word "resident" should not be interpreted as "unit owner" or "association member."

Each member of an association has an investment in the community—its landscape, physical assets and facilities, and its monetary funds. The member's investment is his or her unit price plus the cost of ongoing monthly assessments.

Executive Boards

The executive board is responsible for protecting and enhancing the value of the combined membership's assets. Whether the condo homeowner association is incorporated or not, board members are responsible for the management of a business. Condo association boards are analogous to corporate business boards. They are elected by shareholders (unit owners) to run the corporation (the association). They are elected to operate the community's affairs—to protect and enhance the association's assets and community lifestyle. Board members are volunteers (unlike paid corporate board members) who are willing to take the risk and assume the responsibility of governance because they feel they represent the majority of association members. They feel that they have the ability to do the job, and their majority supporters give them the leeway to do the job as they see fit.

Boards are responsible for the governance of the association according to federal, state, and municipal laws as well as the association's governing documents which include the declaration, bylaws, and resident's

"Unit owners may get their say, but they may not get their way."

manual of policies and procedures. These documents should have been made available to purchasers when an agreement to purchase was signed. Association members are the citizens of a condo community and look to the board for guidance and fair application of association policy. In essence, boards are responsible for protecting the quality of life that was presented to prospective purchasers.

Membership on a board should not be undertaken for the wrong reasons. Seeking a board position should not be about a quest for power and status or the pursuit of a personal agenda. And it definitely should not be pursued by cheating. Board membership is about the leadership and inspiration of a team effort. Effective board governance involves the assumption of many roles. It requires a lot of energy and is not for the weak-willed or faint of heart.

Many associations' members are of the opinion that the board is elected to represent them—in essence, to govern the community according to their individual wishes. They perceive the board election process to be similar to the political format of municipalities and the federal government. If there is any similarity, it is that elected officials to a government or association are responsible to the majority of citizens or unit owners who elected them. If association board members do not satisfy the majority that elected them, they will not get elected for another term.

There will always be minority interest group opinions in condo associations. The minority's opinions should always be heard, but they do not have to result in policy changes that suit their demands. More simply stated, "Unit owners may get their say, but they may not get their way." An association minority group may be hell-bent for a change and never give up its crusade. All the board can do is make a decision, explain it, and then dismiss (ignore) any further challenge. A minority of malcontents can make a lot of noise. It can cause volunteer board members to resign from the board (give up). It can lie, slander, and even commit election forgery to get its way. I served on a board that experienced such criminal behavior. [See Chapter 24 for the whole story.] In most cases, the minority opinion is simply a distraction to be tolerated until the next election.

Many community associations experience Jerry Seinfeld moments such as the "Del Boca Vista Phase III" episode which resulted in the impeachment of Morty Seinfeld and election of Jack Klompus as board president. These moments can end up costing associations a lot of money and bad publicity. Sometimes boards have to draw a line in the sand and say, "Enough is enough." The integrity of the board and its ability to conduct operations and attract good volunteers must be protected from dysfunctional malcontents who cannot live happily in the condominium environment.

Association executive boards usually consist of an odd number (3, 5, or 7) of members, depending on the size of the community. The odd number facilitates a majority decision on issues. Board members can be elected, appointed, or unelected by a majority vote of association members at a special meeting duly called. Board members may be unit owners or not—per the association bylaws. They may be paid or not. All of the election requirements are detailed in the association's governing documents. These documents can be amended at any time and from time to time by a majority vote of a stipulated percentage (usually 50-67%) of association membership.

Along with an odd number of board members, boards can also have an odd mix of personalities, experience, and goals. Having been a board member for twenty-seven years, I think I've seen it all. I've even seen board members resign from a board after only one meeting. I was elected a board member in 1990 and have served nine consecutive terms as the board treasurer of a large association. Long-term tenure on a condo board is a rarity. With twenty-seven consecutive years on a board, I might have a state or national record. I should probably contact the Guinness World Record people.

Community Association Managers

Boards must learn to work with and without an association manager. If a board delegates its authority to a professional manager, the board must act as one in its dealings with the manager. A manager cannot be effective if he or she has to answer to board members acting individually. The board, acting as one, is the manager's boss. It must be careful not to micromanage the manager. Whenever I was interviewed for an association position and found the board to be dysfunctional, I excused myself from the board's consideration. A manager cannot be successful if the board (his boss) is infighting.

There is a big difference between an off-site management company and an on-site manager, especially if the on-site manager also lives in the community. Off-site managers are somewhat restricted by their management company employer as to their degree of involvement in the community. They may be reluctant to be proactive because it can lead to increased liability for decisions made. What can be accomplished with a reluctant "handcuffed" manager and an indecisive board? Not much!

By contrast, an experienced on-site manager is a better boss of an HOA's daily operations and capital projects management. Once the manager is acclimated to the community, he or she can solve or deflect most problematic situations. The board will be spared a lot of anxiety and board meeting hours. In all the communities under my management or guidance, I became known as a professional problem solver.

A manager cannot be effective if he or she has to answer to board members acting individually. The board, acting as one, is the manager's boss

I was an anomaly in the condo industry business, being the board treasurer and manager, simultaneously, of a large condo community for such a long time. I was also a resident owner in the community. Through this experience, I learned to walk the conflict-of-interest tightrope. The community knew me as someone who could run a set of accounting books as well as running a chainsaw. Most of the members in this association knew me to be a jack of all trades and accepted my dual role in the association management hierarchy. After all, I was elected by large majorities to nine consecutive three-year terms as the board treasurer.

However, as a result of my omni-involvement in the community, my determination and perseverance were frequently tested by a disgruntled minority of association members. If I heard it once, I heard it a thousand times over my nine-term tenure in the community: "He shouldn't be board treasurer and manager. It's a conflict of interest." My dual roles as board member and manager were not disallowed by the association's documents. Many S&P 500 Corporations have CEOs who are also board members or even chairman of the board. Potential conflicts of interest must always be disclosed to the association membership. They are perceptions that may never come to fruition in the form of management malfeasance. They must simply be transparent, monitored, and controlled.

In all of the communities that I managed or consulted for, there were always some residents who were not suited to live in a structured condo environment. They just couldn't live in a setting with rules and regulations. Though these character types probably abide by municipal, state, and federal laws, they have a problem with compliance to the rules of a condo association. I guess it is just too up-close and personal for their comfort. It could be because private condo associations don't have their own police force. In other words, the rules are inconsequential if no one can enforce them. That is why I'm not sure if the condo association management model as it exists today is a viable model for the future.

Many baby boomers (the Woodstock generation) do not like being told what to do. In some instances, their early years were all about an anti-authority attitude which may have been emboldened by the use of drugs. If, as a

Many baby boomers do not like being told what to do.

manager, you have to deal with a baby boomer demographic in your association, good luck. You will be severely challenged, especially if they are professionals (doctors, lawyers, business owners, etc.). If they perceive themselves to be part of a protected minority, your challenges will be compounded. A condo association manager must learn to walk a fine line when enforcing the community policies against any self-perceived minorities whether they are gender based, sexual orientation based, race based, religion based, or conservation based (animal lovers or tree huggers). If enforcement is not applied with a tender touch, you will be accused of prejudicial treatment. Believe me, I have had to deal with challenges from all of the aforementioned groups.

Experienced association managers are those who have learned to pick their battles wisely. Almost exclusively, battles that could end up costing the association a lot of money should not be fought. I don't think I was ever suckered into a fight that I wasn't sure I could win. However, managers who are young and inexperienced are generally more impulsive and less able to swallow their pride. Sometimes "biting the bullet" for the benefit of the association, as personally revolting as it may be, is the most unselfish and admirable action. It's that "I lost the battle, but won the war" mentality that usually only comes with age and wisdom.

Chapter 4

MEETINGS 101
HANDS-ON MANAGER STYLE

The most attended condo association meeting I ever experienced was in the spring of 1990. It was a special meeting, called with the intent to reject the community's 1990-1991 fiscal year budget. Over two-thirds of the members (approximately 275 members) were in attendance. That budget was rejected and about one month later, three board members were replaced at the ballot box. I was one of the new board members.

I have learned that most problems are more emotional than substantive and can be solved with common sense and a sense of fair play.

Twenty-five years later, I experienced the second largest attendance at a meeting of the same association. A very small disgruntled minority group put up two board candidates in hopes of stacking the board. Challenges, protests, forged documents, and a police presence made for a very ugly evening. The existing board prevailed, though, and the noisy minority failed. [See Chapter 24 for more details.]

Other than the two aforementioned meetings, most of the meetings I've attended as a board member, manager, or consultant have been sparsely attended. Heck, one association couldn't even achieve the required twenty percent quorum at most of its annual election meetings. That quorum requirement was eventually amended and reduced to ten percent. As a member who has owned a unit in this community for over thirty years, I can tell you the reason for the low voter turnout in one word: apathy. But it's the good kind of apathy. This is a well-run self-managed community with a stellar reputation. The vast majority of association members and residents are happy.

Nonetheless, every once in awhile the shit hits the fan! In most associations there is usually a very noisy minority that clamors for more meetings or more open meetings. Then, after their meeting demands are met, they usually don't even attend the meetings they wanted.

Open or Closed?

Most associations have a mix of meetings throughout the year. Some meetings are open to all owners, and some are just for board members. Sometimes members request an audience at these private board meetings, either to observe or to express a grievance. If the state condo law or the association's governing documents call for all association meetings to be open to all membership, then there better be compliance.

Association meeting policy and procedures run the gamut of possibilities. What works for one association may not work for another. I'm from the camp of: the fewer open meetings the better. If an association's meeting requirements (notice, attendance, minutes, etc.) are properly managed, and the minutes are made available for the membership to review, then the association board members are fulfilling their responsibility. The more people who attend a meeting, the longer it will be. And less will be accomplished.

Taking Charge of a Meeting

There is plenty of published information on meeting procedures (i.e. *Robert's Rules of Order*). It's all an association needs to fulfill its expected meeting requirements. Based on the fact that I have been going to condo meetings for twenty-seven years, I can tell you that effective meetings require:

- ☐ A take charge, no-nonsense president
- ☐ A tight agenda
- ☐ Preparation (homework) by board members
- ☐ Robert's Rules of Order (or acceptable facsimile)
- ☐ Precise minutes of actions taken
- ☐ Minimal chit-chat (agenda drift)

Very few associations have such meetings, but they have to give it their best shot. A board's intent, consistency, and fairness become crucial tangibles when their governance issues are questioned or taken into court.

Some board meetings only take about forty-five minutes to an hour. Others can average two to three hours per meeting. The length of a board meeting has a direct correlation to the personality or nature of the board members themselves. For instance, if a board has an aura of self-confidence and conviction, meetings will be shorter. If a board does not exude confidence and tends to be worrisome or paranoid (i.e., I'm afraid they'll sue us), meetings will be longer. Such a board personality tends to be indecisive about anything, especially controversial issues. A board has to lead the association. It can't be perceived as wishy-washy. A hesitant board is more susceptible to being taken hostage by a quirky minority, and as a result, less is accomplished.

Leading Instead of Following

At one point, I was interviewed for an HOA management position for a large detached-home community that was transitioning from developer control to independent control by association executive board. The nationally known S&P 500 company still controlled the board, and its representative was on the panel that interviewed me.

I didn't get the job. My true colors showed through when I couldn't resist telling the panel that there were a few projects that should be completed at the developer's expense before finalizing the transition.

Since that interview about six years ago, the community has had to correct the problems I exposed, but at the association's expense. The developer escaped what should have been his responsibility. Since the transition the community has also seen a few managers come and go.

Managing Conflict

Once I attended a homeowner association (HOA) manager's seminar in Plymouth Meeting, Pennsylvania. The seminar topic title was "Managing Conflict and Disruptive Behavior." It was well attended (standing room only). The unusually high attendance was an immediate indication that there is a lot of conflict and odd behavior happening in HOAs. The seminar host was a very large HOA management firm headquartered in the Philadelphia area. This is an off-site management company that occasionally places a manager on-site on a part-time basis.

The seminar platform was open forum style where problems were described, experience shared, and resolution paths proposed. The most common conflict discussed was one that occurs between off-site managers and the HOA executive boards. The managers lamented that they attend two to four hour meetings and nothing gets accomplished due to board infighting. And to complicate these matters, these meetings are open to all association members, who inevitably get caught up in the emotion, take sides, and then get rowdy. At one HOA community, board members were escorted to meetings with police protection.

Another hot issue was the management of hoarders and ill or elderly residents who are no longer capable of independent living. When and how should management get involved to protect the health and welfare of adjoining unit owners, residents, or the condo community at large? What are the liability implications?

What did this seminar do for me? It reminded me that times are tough and people are under enormous stress—economic, job-related, physical, emotional, or all of the above. Under such stress, the demand for compliance to HOA policy and procedures by the association manager is very unwelcome. Nonetheless on-site management and a high quality maintenance system nip most problems in the bud.

Joining the Family

In 1989, at the age of forty, I became a father to my first child, Leigh. I was in the delivery room for the Caesarean birth and even volunteered to make the lower abdominal incision. Needless to say, I was not allowed to wield the scalpel.

One year later in 1990, I felt compelled to adopt the Glencreek Condo Association, not realizing at the time that it would all but become another family member, demanding serious attention and requiring much family sacrifice.

Then in 1991 my second daughter, Ruthie, was born and the surgical team still would not let me do the Caesarean cut, even though I had observed the procedure less than two years earlier.

How did I become such a "hands-on" person? I'm pretty sure it came from my dad. He spent a lot of his time and energy on me. I was repeatedly told that the more things in life I could take care of myself, the happier I would be.

Guess what? Twenty-six years after my family responsibilities began, I still believe in the "hands-on" style of management more than ever. In business or at home, it's hard to beat.

Still Want to Be an Association Manager?

The year 2010 was the busiest that I have experienced since I retired from Citigroup in 2002 and entered the world of homeowner association management. Association management was not completely new to me as I had been treasurer of the Glencreek Condo Board for thirteen years at that time.

While maintaining two other associations besides Glencreek, I experienced a year of turmoil and accomplishment. Of note were a complete repaving of one community, a major storm water management project in another, and the never-ending upkeep of Glencreek that included six roof replacements and six major sections of sidewalk. If managing these projects wasn't enough in itself, focusing on

Owners and association boards must choose their battles carefully and expect that compromise will be part of any acceptable resolution.

them was very difficult with the backdrop of board politics and controversy. And believe me, such controversy is never completely avoided by any homeowner association.

I have been called upon through the years to consult with other area associations on resolving controversial issues. Not unlike the circumstances that we have to deal with in our journeys through life, condo controversy can be the result of incompetence, misinterpretation, selfishness, and even fraud.

I have learned that most problems are more emotional than substantive and can be solved with common sense and a sense of fair play. Owners and association boards must choose their battles carefully and expect that compromise will be part of any acceptable resolution.

HOA management can be a very rewarding career path. Professional success and longevity require a background of knowledge and experience in construction, finance, HOA law, insurance, and public relations to mention a few. An even temperament and sense of humor should garnish these technical skills. The future proliferation of HOA communities and the diverse demographic mix of their association membership will make association management even more challenging. I predict that HOA management will eventually be a course of study at most universities and that a license to practice will become a requirement.

A Day in the Life of a Hands-On Manager

About 7:00 a.m. on a Sunday morning, July 25, 2011, I continued with the summer party clean up. I spent most of the morning picking up trash, rearranging pool furniture, cleaning the pool, returning equipment to storage, and packing up rented furniture. It was still pretty hot, mid-morning, and I was joined by volunteers who had done much to help make the party a success.

At noon I rested and had my lunch by the pool. I am not currently a certified lifeguard but I was at one time. I did my training and took my test at the Glencreek pool in the mid-seventies. When I sit at the pool, I watch and could offer help if necessary. Since I know most of the pool attendees I am somewhat aware of potential safety situations. Coincidentally, no lifeguards were available this day.

Violent weather moved in about 2:00 p.m. and my rest was over. I had to scurry to get everyone out of the pool and secure the area. I had just finished when I received a call from City Plaza (another community that I manage) that one of their buildings was struck by lightning and a fire was in progress. I hustled to the scene where there were more fire trucks and ambulances than the Hortonville Fireman's Field Day. I spent about three hours there, helping as much as I could. Mostly, I assured affected residents that insurance companies, restoration companies, and other contractors had already been notified to be on site ASAP.

While wrapping up my responsibilities at City Plaza I received a call from Ash Hill (another community I manage) that two large trees had blown down on vehicles. I immediately called my go-to tree guy, and he said he could be on site in about an hour. Later that evening I checked in on the situation—the tree mess was cleaned up with the wood neatly stacked. I did my last check-in of the day at City Plaza to see how things were going and find out if electricity had been restored to the building.

Finally, I arrived home at about 8:00 p.m. and fielded a few more calls of concern until I hit the sack at 11:00 p.m. I went to sleep thinking about the next day's chore of pavement sealing and striping the office parking lot, wondering what could possibly go wrong with that. There was bound to be some unexpected excitement.

And there was...when one of the residents at Glencreek drove through the safety barriers over the freshly sealed and striped parking lot, dragging the caution tape and six cones behind her big black Cadillac.

Chapter 5

COMMUNICATION

THE KEY TO COOPERATION

Avoiding Email Addiction

Whenever I was interviewed for a prospective condo management or consulting contract, one of the main concerns of the interviewer was how I managed community communications. How did I respond to unit owner concerns? How did I enforce compliance to the association's policy and procedures? How would I correspond with the board members and they to me? These were all legitimate concerns and questions. My answers to these questions went something like this:

"I have an excellent reputation for public relations and communicating with boards and unit owners. I can provide references. I communicate through community newsletters, telephone calls, personal visits or interviews, and if necessary personal letters."

The boards' responses were usually the same, "What about email?" My answer was always, "I'm sorry, but one of my contract stipulations is that I will not accept or send emails, because I don't have a smart phone, laptop, or desktop computer. Spending a few hours every day answering emails, tweets, and texts would diminish my effectiveness and reputation. It's just not my style." I would go on to explain, "Anyone can call me on my cell phone 24/7, and I do not screen my calls. When my phone rings, I answer it. Call the other associations that I manage and see what they say about me."

Being a "tech-luddite" never lost me a prospective management job that I really wanted. When boards gave me a chance, I proved that my old-fashioned communication style was effective. It was honest, straightforward, and refreshing.

One community I managed had an on-site management office and an office administrator who had a reputation for excellence. Once in awhile, I would respond to an email through my administrative assistant and her desktop computer. It was always my last method of communication. My low-tech-or-no-tech philosophy of condo communication has served me well for over twenty-seven years. I'm glad that I'm close to condo industry retirement because, unless there are changes in condo management techniques, the current association off-site "management by email"model will not survive.

Publishing a Newsletter

Newsletters create goodwill while educating and entertaining association members. The larger your community, the more successful your newsletter will be. However, good results can also be accomplished in small communities.

All of the associations that I have managed or consulted for have had some type of community newsletter—monthly, quarterly, or bi-annual. Most are very basic but a few are quite impressive, either paying for themselves (breaking even) or generating a healthy profit.

I am directly involved with a community that has had a monthly newsletter since its inception more than three decades ago. Today it is typically a twelve-page edition with infrequent special inserts. It's produced in an on-site management office with a computer, scanner, and color copier. My assistant is paid $120 per month to produce it. All sorts of information that enhances the community lifestyle appears in the newsletter. It is financed through ad sales. Most of the ads are bought by the various community service providers.

This newsletter generates approximately $10,000 per year in ad revenue and costs about $5,000 to produce (labor and materials). The net profit helps fund many of the community's social and recreational events. When it comes to community newsletters, it doesn't get any better.

If there's no management staff to produce a newsletter, a volunteer with a computer can accomplish the task. Copying can be done at an office supply store. I can't imagine an association that would not spend the money to fund such a valuable service.

Several of the articles appearing in this book are one association's reprints. Over the life of this association the monthly newsletter has served as an informal chronological history of association activity. As such, it has become a valuable asset.

Controlling Association Websites

Websites that are not strictly controlled by condo boards can quickly turn into disasters. They can undermine community spirit and create a marketing nightmare. In my opinion, a condo association should never host a website that allows association members or community residents to post their thoughts and ideas. Such a site will not be a pretty sight.

There are numerous ways to channel criticism, suggestions, or new ideas to the board or management without harming the perception and public relations of the community. Most of my experience with community websites has not been favorable to anyone involved with their operation.

Chapter 6

KNOW YOUR COMMUNITY

Condo associations and their communities have a personality based on their demographic or set of features that set them apart from their industry peers. In associations that I managed or consulted for, I was always quick to identify the features that promoted success and, more importantly, the "personality" features that were going to cause big problems if not corrected.

Private Property: Please Keep Out

One association community I managed was concerned that they were not being taken seriously as a private community. This association had a private drive that was not respected by outsiders. People used the drive as a shortcut. Speeding was an ever-present danger from these outsiders, not to mention the increased wear and tear on the pavement. The sidewalk along the street was also being used by outside walkers, joggers, and dogs.

I advised the board of this community that if they wanted to be recognized and respected as a private community they had to act like one. These are the steps I advised them to take in order to achieve privacy and regain control of the street and sidewalks.

- [ ] Install a community entrance with signage, landscaping, lighting, and a flagpole.
- [ ] Install additional "private community" signage citing municipal code sections.
- [ ] Install two speed bumps at strategic locations.
- [ ] Notify the local police department of the private street status concerns.
- [ ] Clean up a storm water drainage swale that was immediately adjacent to, and visible from, the street.
- [ ] Improve landscaping along the street.
- [ ] Install back entrance signage, albeit on a smaller scale.

All of my recommendations were enacted and accomplished new-found privacy for the community.

Signs of the Times

Another community I managed had an identity crisis—literally. Each building in this eleven-building community (102 units) was once identified by a large unlit wooden sign that was screwed on the front of the building and had the building name on it (i.e., Aspen). After twenty years or so, these signs had become so dirty and deteriorated that the building names were unreadable. Units within the building were identified by small unit numbers at the doorways, which were similarly deteriorated. I improved building and unit identification by:

- ☐ Removing old wooden signs
- ☐ Installing high quality and architecturally appealing signposts in front of each building with reflective signs indicating building unit numbers (i.e., Units 101-112)
- ☐ Landscaping around signposts
- ☐ Installing new unit numbers on new color-coordinated plaques that were attached at each door threshold near the door lamplights

Buildings were now recognizable by their unit numbers within them and were clearly visible to visitors, contractors, service providers, ambulances, and police.

Fragile: Handle with Care

The last community that I managed and lived in was initially neglected during its first ten years after converting from rental apartments to condos. When the bottom fell out in 1990, the association had only $36,000 in its capital reserve fund. Most certainly, this was not enough cash for a large condo community with several expensive amenities to maintain.

When I got involved with the community that year, I quickly realized that just about everything you could think of had to be done. That "everything" was, is, and will have to be done for the foreseeable future.

Chapter 7

DO IT YOURSELF
OR NOT?

Modern condo communities and those coming online may
not have been constructed with the facilities (buildings or
equipment) that enable self-management. Developers consider
it expensive and unnecessary—it eats into their profits. This
means that many condo associations are at the mercy of off-
site management companies. Successful self-managed condo
communities are the gold standard for condo management,
as far as I am concerned. At this point, I don't know if they
will eventually proliferate or become extinct. I'm sure that
by now, readers know which management style I recommend.

On-Site Maintenance

A condo board cannot self-manage a large community unless
its maintenance staff and management office have good equipment (adequate for all seasons) and a maintenance facility.
When my dad was a superintendent of highways in Upstate
New York, his most frequent refrain when criticized by the
local taxpayers was, "In order for me to do a good job, you
gotta give me good equipment." I never forgot that.

When I took over the management of the condo community in which I live, I began to acquire the equipment necessary to do a good job. Luckily, I had a cooperative board that trusted my judgment and enabled me to get what I needed. Over time, we were able to purchase:

☐ Two new pickup trucks with toolboxes
☐ New utility wagon with tailgate
☐ New tractor with bucket, forks, and an enclosed cab (for winter time)
☐ Four new heavy-duty, six-speed snow blowers
☐ Four backpack leaf blowers
☐ Two 3500 PSI power washers
☐ Two chainsaws (one large and one small)
☐ Two water pumps (2" and 4")
☐ Scaffolding
☐ A motorized parking line spray painter
☐ Various small power tools

Consequently, the maintenance staff could do just about everything. The maintenance supervisor and two-man staff had a combined sixty years of experience in the community. In addition to maintaining the common area facilities and amenities, they also were available to unit owners to perform billable jobs inside the units. Annual revenues from this in-house maintenance program were approximately $60,000 which included a reasonable profit margin. In case you are wondering, our hourly billing rate was half the prevailing local service rates. It was and is the best deal in town, and residents take advantage of it.

Outside Service Providers

Without in-house maintenance, the condo association must try to keep track of (and control) outside service providers. This can be very difficult.

Unmonitored, the service providers who work in a condo association community can wreck it. Generally speaking, outside service providers do not understand the condominium concept—nor do they care. In addition to cable, satellite, and utility companies, these providers can include:

- ☐ Carpenters
- ☐ Carpet installers and cleaners
- ☐ Insulation installers
- ☐ Plumbers
- ☐ Electricians
- ☐ Painters
- ☐ Drywall installers
- ☐ Tile installers
- ☐ Exterminators
- ☐ Roofers
- ☐ Brick masons

These service providers get a call from a unit owner to come to do this or that, and once they are paid, that's the end of their involvement with the community. Even though condo unit owners are required by their governing documents to get approval for their repairs or renovations, many don't comply. In most instances, condo boards or the manager are not informed that service providers have worked in the community until someone witnesses a violation and reports it. For example, a unit owner may have a new air conditioning unit installed, but the method of installation is not compliant with the association's architectural specifications. When such situations arise, they are difficult to undo and cause a lot of controversy.

In the worst cases, unit owners surreptitiously invite contractors into their units to perform work that is not allowed in the community. In other words, they're trying to pull a fast one. When this happens, the sly unit owners (like chameleons) suddenly turn into ignoramuses saying, "I didn't know it wasn't allowed."

Off-Site vs. On-Site Management

Condo boards with off-site managers have a difficult time maintaining and controlling unapproved service providers working in their communities. One commonly used defense is to install community entrance signage that instructs service providers to check in with the manager through a phone call or visit to the manager's office. Email or text notification doesn't cut it, because the work may get done before such messages are checked or answered. Unfortunately, the first excuse the manager will get from an unauthorized service provider is, "I didn't notice the sign."

Outside service providers don't understand the nuances of common and limited elements and responsibility boundaries in condo communities.

I repeat, outside service providers do not understand that the association has a vested interest in the integrity of the building (its infrastructure). They might think your condo community is an apartment complex. They don't understand the nuances of common and limited elements and responsibility boundaries in condo communities.

Self-managed condo communities with a management office and maintenance personnel on site do a much better job of patrolling and controlling service providers. Go figure. Their on-site staff just cares more. Even so, shit happens!

Before I became the manager of a large association in 2003, the previous manager was lax in controlling the community's service providers. Here's a specific case in point. A nationally known Fortune 500 company was the only cable TV provider in town and of course, the condo community. A company that has a monopoly on a necessary service is sitting in the catbird's seat. Such situations are prone to arrogance and abuse.

To compound this troubling situation, the company was so busy growing that it had to hire subcontractors to service their clients. The subcontractors, who were a step removed from corporate oversight, were out of control. On several occasions over the years, physical confrontation was just a nose length away, and the only thing between me and a jail sentence for bringing a smart-ass service provider into line was the mental vision of my young daughters' angelic faces.

In the spring of 2005, I'd had enough aggravation from this company and its subcontractors. I personally visited their local service facility and stood in their typical snake-like line that extended out the front door. When I finally got to the service window, it was hard to hide the steam coming from my ears.

The robot-like window teller politely asked, "How can I help you, Sir?"

I said, "I need to speak to the local operations manager."

She said, "That's not what this line is for."

And I said, "It is now! I'm Mr. Rosenberger, and unless you get me the manager, this line is gonna get a lot longer."

Surprisingly, she stepped away from the window and disappeared into the back room.

Shortly, a side door opened and a gentleman appeared, asking, "Mr. Rosenberger?" He introduced himself and took me to his office. He politely listened to my exposé of his company's subcontractors and the quality of their work to date in my community. I presented him with a ten-page punch list of grievances and installation problems. He listened well and took my unexpected visit very seriously. He could tell that my tenacity in getting the problem resolved hadn't dissipated over the width of the thirty-inch desk between us. He asked that I allow him some time to investigate the matter.

I responded, "I want the ten-page punch list completed by the end of summer," and said good-bye.

It was only a couple of weeks later that the cable company manager called me. He told me that there would be a special crew dedicated to working full-time until the punch list was completed. He also said that his company allocated $20,000 for the repairs. Except for a few minor glitches and misunderstandings during that summer of work, the project was completed to my satisfaction.

Earlier in this chapter I listed fourteen different types of service providers who have to report and get approval from the manager (me) in the community where I live. Think about what I had to do just to bring one service provider's work into compliance. I could tell more stories about them all, but that alone would require another book.

Chapter 8

CONDOS AND LAWYERS AND LAWS, OH MY!

Association Rules and Regs

The originator of the old adage, "Rules are made to be broken," must have had condominium living in mind. However, there is a big difference between breaking rules intentionally and breaking them unintentionally. When a lack of common sense leads to gross negligence of judgment, then community

In my opinion, the less one has to talk to lawyers or about lawyers the better.

violations tend to seem intentional rather than unintentional.

Many community associations do not have police to enforce rule violations. Consequently, it's difficult to enforce traffic and other violations in private communities. That's exactly why residents need to hold themselves to a higher standard—the standard of common sense and respect for community and neighbors. Without an association police force, residents must police themselves and each other with the help of management.

Most folks accept that there are specific rules and fees for admittance to local public pools and country clubs. And most townships have ordinances and codes that control pets, human health, and the condition of your property. Condo owner associations have rules and regulations that address the same issues. While this is generally accepted by most people, some condo owners repeatedly complain and try to skirt the rules of their association membership.

Why are rules that are similar to your local township governance considered offensive and a violation of personal freedoms in condo associations? Do people move to condos to escape societal rules and standards? I say the whimsical phrase "common sense is not that common" could apply to a lot of odd condominium living happenings, but it cannot be accepted as an excuse.

Remember, lack of respect for community rules will inevitably lead to more rules and more enforcement procedures. If residents want fewer rules, then they must hold themselves to higher standards—the standards of common sense, responsibility and respect for their neighbors.

Legal Issues

In my opinion, the less one has to talk *to* lawyers or *about* lawyers the better. Therefore the time and space I devote to legal issues will be fairly brief.

I haven't spent much time in the presence of lawyers during the course of my life. Hell—even my divorce attorney told me that my divorce was the simplest that he had ever seen to date. I was married for a little over twenty-five years. And even though my wife also used the same attorney, the divorce only cost the both of us a total of $800 dollars. After the divorce we still lived in the house together for two more years for the sake of our daughters, until they graduated from high school and headed for West Point. So really—how difficult was I to get along with?

Well, when you are a community manager or board member, you are exposed to people getting under your skin. My advice to managers and board members is to keep your association out of situations that might necessitate the pursuit of legal advice. Be proactive and conduct the association's operations in such a way as to avoid confrontations with owners and service providers. Remember, most problems are perceived and not real.

Look Before You Leap

Recently, I attended a Community Association Institute (CAI) seminar on dispute resolution in the condominium communities. It was very informative about how to avoid problems that lead to frivolous but expensive litigation. I was astonished at the amount of money that associations budget for legal expense.

Residents or unit owners who need dispute resolution would be wise to look at their association governing documents (declaration, bylaws, rules, and regulations) before leaping into an attorney's office. If emotions are running high, a calm reading and understanding of the governing documents could save a lot of time and money, and at a minimum prevent hard feelings.

The best way to avoid the urge to initiate a legal action against the association (in essence suing yourself) is to read its governing documents. The old saying, "Put your mind in gear before you put your mouth in motion," would be wise advice for anyone considering a lawsuit. Remember, the legal profession is a business profession, and the best way to get business is to tell people what they want to hear.

Know When to Hold 'Em

Nothing will lower the image and market value of a condominium community more than a reputation for never-ending legal challenges. Pick your battles wisely. In other words, pick only the battles you are positive you can win. Usually, if you win, the losing party absorbs the legal costs. Don't feel the need to consult with the association attorney until you hear from the opposition attorney. The atmosphere prior to, during, and after a legal issue is filled with bluffing. Uncontrolled emotions and high-strung personalities lead to legal battles. Patience, compromise, and the use of peer pressure (member to member) have been my most valuable negotiating tools over the years.

In twenty-seven years, I have only had to appear before the district justice a few times to solve an association issue. I won every case and only used an attorney on one occasion. Generally speaking, district justices are not very well versed in condo law. If they have to hear a case, here is what concerns them and what they ask defendants and plaintiffs to clarify:

1. Has the association—through its manager or board— abided by the association's governing documents and/or state condominium act?

2. Does the association apply its rules and regulations in a fair and non-discriminatory manner?

If an association can satisfy the judge or jury in these two procedures, it will probably win its case.

Know When to Fold 'Em

Don't use attorneys for the collection of condo assessments in arrears. They are terribly expensive. Sometimes it can be effective to use an attorney and his letterhead to send a scary letter to the member in arrears. If such a bluff does not jump-start a negotiation, end the attorney engagement for the issue. In states like Pennsylvania, a civil lien is automatic when a unit owner fails to pay assessments. Nevertheless, I still file a civil lien for the collection of a debt with the district justice to make the collection process more intimidating to the delinquent unit owner.

If your condo documents call for acceleration of assessments, don't hesitate to institute the process. This allows the association to file the lien for the dues that are currently in arrears as well as all dues that will be incurred through the end of the fiscal year. Managing the collection process through the district justice office is usually effective and inexpensive, and the cost of filing liens is recoverable from the delinquent party.

Before an association initiates any formal collections process, have a board member appointee or the manager talk to the delinquent in person—not email. If the situation is tense, it would be wise to be accompanied by a witness. This method worked for me, sometimes very unexpectedly. Perhaps I had just the right mix of compassion and intimidation.

I never budgeted more than $1,000 per year for legal expense in any of the associations under my management. That is, until the years following an election-related crime that was perpetrated against one of my associations. That ended up costing about $15,000 to clean up. In all of my other years of management, the annual legal expense was less than budgeted, and in some years it was zero. Very infrequently, an association may have to consult with an attorney to amend the association declaration or bylaws. Only attorneys can formulate the appropriate legalese, so use one.

Always have an experienced condo association attorney at your disposal. If he or she cannot solve the problem in an efficient manner, cut your losses and dispose of that attorney (figuratively speaking).

Chapter 9

RISKY BUSINESS?

Insurance and Risk Management

Whether it's related to the condo industry or not, most people over-insure in a variety of ways. It's natural to want to protect yourself against a perceived risk of loss. Many people buy life insurance as an investment. Why? Because insurance salespeople are more successful if they sell insurance without calling it insurance.

Strong board oversight and a trusted insurance agent are an association's best weapons against liability lawsuits.

Generally speaking, life insurance is a terrible investment. But insurance salespeople know your hot buttons when it comes to fear of the unknown. I was employed as a financial consultant for Citigroup Smith Barney, and I am quite familiar with the mind games that "trusted financial advisors" play. Although I was licensed to sell life insurance, I never attempted to sell a single policy.

Don't Over-Insure

Most people over-insure their vehicles, especially old ones (vehicles not people). After a vehicle is five years old or has traveled 100,000 miles, owners should reduce or eliminate collision coverage, which usually accounts for half the insurance premium. If I have to tell you why, you've never traded in an old vehicle.

The more fearful, insecure, careless, or accident-prone among us buy service plans (a type of insurance) for new jewelry, appliances, etc. This is protection for something minor which is not likely to happen. But such service plans are often the most lucrative aspect of a merchandise sale (for the merchant).

The need for all types of insurance is dependent upon one's perception of his or her human nature, self-confidence, and tolerance for risk. A condo association has all degrees of risk takers among its membership. Some are risk-averse worrywarts while others are self-confident daredevils. In order to satisfy the needs of all types of members, the association has to purchase just the right amount of insurance.

My experience has shown me that most condo associations over-insure because they misunderstand the real risks and real values in their communities. For example, if your condo community is low density (spread out) and is not in a tornado, earthquake, or flood zone, the likelihood of an event occurring that would wipe out the entire community is low. Nonetheless, many associations insure against the worst possible event and not the most probable event. Insurance companies make millions getting clients to insure against what they know is not likely to happen.

When it comes to purchasing insurance, your best ally is an insurance agent you can trust as much as a good brother. Such an agent should be knowledgeable about the nuances of condo communities. Many agents are not. Hopefully, your agent is one who is satisfied with a reasonable commission and not trying to make a killing. If the largest, most expensive home in your town is a waterfront mansion owned by an insurance salesman, I would think twice before becoming one of his clients.

Risk Exposure

Basically, there are two ways to deal with risk exposure: risk financing (insurance) and risk control. Very few, if any, associations self-fund their insurance protection. It would seem impossible, considering the level of expertise and lack of continuity of condo boards. Therefore, the only alternative is to purchase insurance in the open market.

Most associations do not have their own personnel and are managed by off-site management companies who secure and supervise contractors and service providers to maintain the community. Consequently, insurance losses from personnel problems are not a concern.

Condo associations usually need to purchase three types of insurance: property, liability, and fidelity bonds. While carrying such insurance coverage, boards must also focus on risk avoidance and control. They must try to reduce exposure to the most prevalent risk situations in their communities. Risk control is about preventing losses, limiting losses, or transferring losses to a third party (another contractor). Risk financing will be consistently less expensive if, at the same time, the association's insurance carrier believes that the board and manager are conscientious about controlling the risk exposure (producing consistently low loss experience rates).

Property Insurance

Property (building and facilities) replacement insurance has to be purchased for amounts that cover the current replacement cost of the assets. There can be a big difference between market values and replacement cost. Remember the real estate market crash of 2008? Generally speaking, market values were much lower than replacement costs at that time. You've got to determine the true replacement cost of the original building construction components. This requires a methodical process involving the help of a building contractor or engineer. If this is done correctly, property insurance is an area where associations can save insurance premium dollars.

Liability Insurance

Liability insurance is another need. It's difficult to get a handle on the amount of liability insurance that should be purchased by a condo association. It seems like the more liability coverage carried by an association, the more it's likely to be sued for. Liability arises from negligence in decision making by board members, community residents, visitors, and service providers. Contractors and service providers should always be required to provide their certificates of proof of insurance to do work in an association community to minimize the liability from that source.

In addition, condo board members and managers must constantly be alert to liability exposure. Big egos can cause overreactions to tense situations. Elderly residents can make bad decisions about when or how to travel in winter weather. Contractors might take short cuts to increase profits.

Self-managed associations with responsible boards usually do a better job at limiting insurance claims, thus lowering premiums. It's because on-site management is more up close and personal and is more apt to nip problems in the bud. Off-site management companies can be out of touch with their communities, especially during the winter months when walking inspections are cold, dangerous, and infrequent. Strong board oversight and a trusted insurance agent are an association's best weapons against liability lawsuits.

Fidelity Bonds

A fidelity bond, usually in the amount of one year's budget, covers loss or theft of association funds. It should cover all association employees or board members who have access to association funds. A fidelity bond is a requirement for condo associations that seek to be FHA qualified for mortgage loans. This type of insurance is inexpensive.

Lowering the Cost of Insurance

One of the main ways that condo associations can decrease their insurance cost is to raise their policy deductibles. The higher the deductible, the lower the annual premium will be. In some states, the unmet portion of an association deductible can be passed back to the individual association member(s) who incurred damage, regardless of cause or culpability. If this is your association's case, members should be required to purchase loss assessment insurance. This is coverage for the unmet deductible passed back to members. Maximum loss assessment coverage only has to be equal to the association's master policy deductible, and such coverage is inexpensive.

A unit owner can avoid the liability for the association's deductible cost by purchasing insurance to cover all losses not covered by the association's policy. This includes costs due to deductibles. The cost of insuring against an association's deductible of $5,000 is minimal.

What Unit Owners Need to Know About Insurance

As a condo owner, how do you know who is responsible for insuring what? Association boards and members must be clear where insurance responsibilities lie. Typically, when a condo unit is newly constructed, the association is responsible for insuring the unit as offered for sale. That includes the exterior and the building structure, as well as building services such as electrical wiring, plumbing, gas lines, etc. It also includes carpeting and other floor coverings, drywall, paint, cabinets and items of a similar nature. In essence, the association is responsible for insuring the "building" part of a new unit. For a newly built unit, the unit owner policy will cover personal property, liability, loss of use, and owner loss assessment, if purchased.

One thing to keep in mind is that most people make changes of some sort after they move in. It could be as simple as a fresh coat of paint or it could be something more involved like new floor coverings, a new kitchen, or remodeling of the entire unit. In each and every case, when you make changes to your unit, the responsibility for insuring the value of those changes rests with the unit owner, not the association. Those upgrades become the responsibility of the unit owner to insure under improvements and betterments coverage. Most unit owners' policies include some basic amount of coverage, for example $2,500 or $5,000. That is not very much coverage, especially if major changes have been made to your unit, like a new kitchen.

Since the cost of repairing or replacing past alterations continues to increase over time, and since unit owners tend not to remember to report the cost of alterations to their insurance company, I recommend each unit owner purchase a higher limit than what is already included in the basic policy. To arrive at the approximate limit, make a list of everything that has been done to the unit and the approximate cost. Then add at least $5,000 as a safety cushion.

Prior to upgrading a unit, notify the association board and the insurance carrier. Don't be afraid to get "down and dirty" with your insurance agent. There are no dumb questions. Make your agent talk to you so you completely understand your coverage. Make sure you are adequately covered—no more, no less.

From the Manager's Desk: Furnace Rooms

When I was working at Glencreek one day, I noticed that several units in the community had hazardous fire conditions in the furnace rooms adjacent to the patios. More specifically, I found furnace rooms with extreme clutter, including combustible materials touching or in close proximity to hot water heaters (pilot lights), hot pipes, and electric wiring. Such conditions cannot be allowed to exist. Other units within these buildings were potential innocent victims. It's important for residents to inspect their furnace rooms and, if necessary, clean them up in a manner that would satisfy a township fire code inspector. In other words: no combustible materials such as paint, paint thinner, gasoline, oil, paper, cardboard, cloths, broom bristles, etc., should be stored in the furnace room.

As always, we can expect that there will be those residents who don't read the newsletters and will not realize the error of their ways. So in their travels, the maintenance staff will need to be inspecting furnace rooms. Ultimately, maintenance and/or management will make the final determination as to what goes and what stays in the furnace room. It's a matter of common sense enhancement regarding this issue.

Chapter 10

SHOW ME THE MONEY
THE BASICS

The financial management of a condo association is probably the easiest function to accomplish by the manager or board of directors. Then again, that is me speaking as a licensed CPA...

In a nutshell, financial management has two main facets: budgeting and accounting. Once the association annual budget is approved by the board (and the association membership if the bylaws stipulate their approval), it is enacted. For the ensuing fiscal year, the actual receipt of monthly assessments and disbursement of funds for operating expenses and capital reserve fund contributions are tracked and compared to the budget on a monthly and year-to-date basis. Item surpluses or deficiencies are noted and discussed by the manager and the board. At that point, adjustments may have to be made. (Wasn't that easy?)

Budgeting

A condo association budget is usually prepared by the association manager with input from the board members. It is an estimate of the association's income (revenue) and expenses for the entire upcoming fiscal year, and it is broken down on a monthly basis. Budgeted revenue amounts will remain fairly constant, because the assessments for a fixed number of units are quite predictable. Budget expense categories also remain fairly constant throughout the life of a fully phased-in community. Most expenses can be projected as to the month that they will be incurred. Nevertheless, even a well-thought-out budget may still have some random expenses (surprises).

Even a well thought out budget will have some random surprises.

As a licensed but non-practicing CPA, I prepared the proposed budgets for the associations under my management. When I prepared budgets, I always paid attention first to the expense side of the financial statement. Accounting instructors would view my budgeting technique as a combination of zero-based and historical trend budgeting methodologies. Since this book is not a technical instruction manual, I will not explain these budgeting methods. Suffice it to say that most associations, whether they realize it or not, use the historical trend budgeting method. Its name is self-explanatory. The zero-based budgeting method is more appropriate for brand new associations, but it can also be used effectively as a check and balance of the historical trend method. It requires one to analyze the reasons why funds have to be disbursed. This is because association community circumstances change from time to time and for various reasons.

With associations that I managed, I knew the approximate annual operating cost of each association when all of the budgeted expenses were totaled. Then all I had to be certain of was that the previous year's actual revenue was equal to or greater than the newly budgeted operating cost.

If the revenue was at least five percent greater than estimated expenses, I recommended to the board that monthly assessments could remain unchanged. If the previous year's revenue fell short of the upcoming year's budgeting expenses, I re-analyzed my budget assumptions. If they were correct, I told the board that monthly assessments should be increased to cover expenses and break even. Often I recommended they increase assessments at least two to five percent to "cover their butts." This system worked successfully for me for twenty-seven years, and my reputation for holding to budgets was impeccable.

Accounting

In my opinion, association finances can be tracked with "pencil and paper" accounting. Property management companies tend to make the accounting process for associations more complicated than it should be. Perhaps it helps them justify a higher management fee. In this age of electronic processing, all kinds of cash receipts reports can be generated, often confusing to boards and managers. The reporting process may be accelerated, but the report understanding is not. Too much information can be confusing.

On the income side, when it comes to the collection and accounting for monthly condo fees, there is no need for lengthy and complicated reports. It's simple. *The same fees for the same units come in once a month for twelve months and that's it!* The monthly assessments are collected by drop-off, mail, or direct debit. In larger associations the direct debit process greatly facilitates the revenue collection exercise.

All assessments are considered earned as each month passes and are accrued on the books. With "can-do" accounting software packages, it's automatic. What about delinquent accounts that owe assessments in arrears? First of all, that is not an accounting problem. The collection of delinquent assessments is a different task and was discussed in Chapter 8: Condos and Lawyers, and Laws, Oh My!

On the expense side, most associations only disburse about ten to twenty checks per month during their busy season, depending on their climate. For example, December through March in the northeast United States are usually limited transaction months, with snow and ice removal being the main operational activity. Most construction and landscaping activities take place between April and October.

Once again, ten to twenty checks per month is "paper and pencil" accounting. In my universe of condo management (three or four properties), an old-fashioned, thirteen-column spreadsheet did the job. For "techies" a simple accounting package will suffice. This type of accounting certainly isn't rocket science.

It's easy to categorize and summarize the revenue and expense transactions of a typical association. And it doesn't get any more complicated for large associations with more units, either. It is still the same-old-same-old every month. Adding in more units simply means summarizing more data. When you have summarized the actual and/or accrued (earned but not received or incurred but not paid) revenue and expenses, what do you do with these figures? Compare them on a monthly basis to their budgeted categories and analyze the variances (over/under).

Association Funds

Condo association accounting typically involves the management of two separate funds: an operating fund and a capital reserve fund. The operating fund is established for the daily operations of the association. The capital reserve fund is established for the infrequent replacement of major infrastructure (big ticket items such as roofs). The budgeting process for the capital reserve fund is basically the same as that used for the operating fund, as previously discussed. First, determine the large replacement costs to be incurred and estimate when those costs have to be funded. Then, simply budget the necessary funds on a monthly and annual basis in order to accumulate the total amount necessary for each replacement item by the time it needs to be replaced.

Reserve Studies

Determining when a capital reserve item has to be replaced is the tricky part. Unless the manager or board member has extensive construction experience, this task is best left to a reserve study specialist. Such a specialist is usually employed by an engineering firm. But be careful. Such studies can cost from $3,000 to $50,000 depending on the extent of the community's building units and facilities. There is a lot of room for profit in capital reserve studies. However, if done correctly with reasonable cost replacement estimates, these studies are a valuable tool for the most uninformed manager or boards.

Let me explain the nature of the "Reserve Study Beast." At its best, the reserve study helps the association board fulfill their fiduciary responsibility, thus avoiding the liability exposure to charges of poor planning. The reserve study will also make auditors and lenders more comfortable with the financial statements. It can be a blueprint for understanding the financial implications of large infrastructure replacement projects. At its worst, a professional reserve study can be an overanalyzed ultra-conservative, bloated estimate of future replacement costs that leads to overfunding. Capital reserve overfunding occurs when present association members are assessed too much for the benefit of future association members.

Here's the problem: I have yet to see a reserve study that wasn't overfunded.

Here is the biggest problem with reserve studies: I have yet to see one that wasn't at least thirty-three percent overfunded. Reserve study specialists are more conservative than a CPA with a hat and wing-tip shoes! Why? Because they have liability exposure if their future cost estimates end up being too low. So they make sure they cover *their* butts. Think about it. They don't really know when an association will do the recommended work. They also don't know what the materials market will be, who will do the work, or how much a naïve board will be billed by the contractors. Reserve specialists may be well intentioned and their analyses correct, but their cost projections are usually ridiculously high. I never saw a reserve study budget that could not be trimmed substantially.

My own construction knowledge enabled me to avoid conducting full-blown reserve studies most of the time. Only late in my condo career did I have to submit to a reserve study. It was a Federal Housing Administration (FHA) lending approval requirement which condo associations must complete for the community to be eligible for FHA loans. Aggressive realtors tend to push for these studies because FHA qualified loans will enable faster sales. On a side note, FHA mortgages have the lowest interest rates. Such low rates attract all potential buyers but also a higher percentage of buyers who can't afford anything else. Less affluent buyers who just make ends meet every month are not a good demographic for an upscale condo community. The real estate crash of 2008 proved that people buy first and then discover they do not have adequate funds for long-term real estate ownership.

In Other Words...

To summarize, the financial management process is simply about accounting for actual expenses versus budgeted expenses. This process takes place in the operating and capital reserve funds. Don't let the experts tell you that it is extremely difficult. It is just about addition, subtraction, and percentages.

Chapter 11

SHOW ME THE MONEY

ACCOUNTABILITY

Who Would Buy Into a Community Association If...

- ☐ It had a history of large, unexpected special assessments?
- ☐ It showed negative equity on the balance sheet of the financial statements?
- ☐ It couldn't manage its daily operations within budget?
- ☐ There were low or no capital replacement reserves?
- ☐ The monthly assessment delinquency rate was ten to twenty percent of gross assessments?
- ☐ There was a history of large legal expenses?
- ☐ The manager turnover rate was abnormally high?
- ☐ Association leadership could not attract good volunteers to fill vacant board positions?
- ☐ The board members and/or manager didn't have a good understanding of the governing documents?

Prior to any purchase of property in any community with a homeowners' association, all of the above questions should be discussed and understood by the buyer. Information sources include realtors, other residents, the community manager, or a board member. Don't simply rely on one realtor.

Audits

Most large condo associations (100 or more units) are required by their governing documents to have an annual audit by an independent CPA firm. It may even be required by state condo laws. An audit is an external verification of the accuracy and completeness of the association's financial statements. It can also be a check-up of the association's accounting system and internal controls. It serves to assure all association members that the board and manager are fulfilling their fiduciary responsibilities. In other words, your real estate investment in the association is being protected in an efficient and responsible manner.

Audits have become tedious and expensive, because audit procedures and requirements are fairly uniform across the spectrum of industries from large to small. Smaller businesses (condo associations) suffer because of the sins of the large corporations, banks, mortgage companies, and Wall Street. Condo associations have limited funds, and it is hard to justify the cost of an audit in their budgets. About the only thing an association can do to lower its auditing fee is to keep a pristine set of books. Having everything in order on the day the auditor walks into the management office can save some bucks, because helping the auditors in any way you can lessens the amount of time devoted to the audit.

If your association's governing documents require an annual audit, it had better be done. If an audit is only required by your bylaws or declaration, there is a way to eliminate the requirement by amending your documents. Only as an extreme budget trimming measure should the audit be eliminated. Sometimes even having an annual audit won't be enough to satisfy boards' or managers' worst critics. Once, as a board treasurer, I was accused of having the auditors in my back pocket. In order to take the heat off myself and the board, we decided to hire another CPA auditor to audit the auditors. This absurd undertaking ended up costing our association an additional $800. The second auditor apologized to me several times as he felt guilty about taking the engagement in the first place. [See Appendix B for his concluding letter.] As a CPA myself, I never liked being checked by other CPAs. But I still felt that an annual audit that would verify the accuracy of my work would make me feel good. It is the audit cost that made me ill.

Direct Debit Programs

How does the direct debit system work? The unit owner gives their bank account and bank routing numbers to the community's management office, and those numbers are entered into the system. Then, once a month, the assessment amount is electronically deducted from the owner's bank account. It appears on his bank statement as a debit, just as if he wrote a check. Unit owners do not need computers to enable this transaction to take place.

Ideally, managers would like to see all unit owners use the direct debit system for paying their monthly assessment. It is easier, less expensive, and more accurate because the following partial list of issues can be avoided:

- ☐ Wrong amount on check
- ☐ Numerals and words on check don't match
- ☐ Unsigned checks
- ☐ Assessment checks mailed to other service providers
- ☐ Wet checks with smeared ink
- ☐ Envelope flaps stuck to checks
- ☐ Ripped checks
- ☐ Lost checks
- ☐ Post-dated checks
- ☐ Forgotten payments (memory issues)

Direct debit processing is less expensive for homeowners and community associations alike, because there is no need for envelopes or stamps, no late charges, no office time for correcting errors, fewer NSF charges, no mistakes, and improved cash flow.

For the benefit of their community associations, unit owners should consider signing up. If they don't like it, they can cancel at any time.

The Community Association Treasurer

Each year when association boards elect their officers, no one ever wants to be the treasurer. Why? Because it is an enormous responsibility, and the person who is elected has to know what he is doing. Diverting association assets from their intended purpose is a very real possibility in any community association. (I've attended seminars on the financial horror stories.) Because of this, it's critical that the treasurer of an association have a squeaky clean financial background and a reputation for prudent financial practices. The safety and liquidity of association assets are essential to community associations. It's important for treasurers to know how to invest homeowners' funds to insure their protection.

A condominium association treasurer is responsible for maintaining the finances and ensuring the financial stability of the association. He or she is the financial voice of the board and liaison to brokers, agents, bankers, auditors, and CPAs. The job includes a number of duties and responsibilities:

- [ ] Preparation of the annual operating budget
- [ ] Maintaining association accounts and records, insurance, investments, assessments, reserves, and tax returns
- [ ] Understanding the association's financial statements including assets, liabilities, members' equity, operating and reserve fund accounting, working capital, special projects, and statement of cash flows.
- [ ] Preparation of reports to the board
- [ ] Daily bookkeeping
- [ ] Selection of a CPA for conducting an audit

What Does the Budget Mean for Owners?

After one open association meeting, I was approached by several residents who suggested that I publish an excerpt from my presentation in the association's newsletter. Following is an expanded version of that presentation segment that shows unit owners' monthly costs (as covered by their monthly assessments) for various (but not all) services. These numbers were based on the current operating budget at the time.

BUDGET ITEM	COST/OWNER
Landscaping	38.89
Maintenance Staff Wages & P/R Taxes	18.93
Trash Removal	8.40
Misc. Common Area Repairs	4.44
Snow Removal	4.89
Maintenance Group Health Insurance	5.11
Pool Expense	2.44
Exterminating	0.67
Office Wages & P/R Taxes	6.47
Manager Salary & P/R Taxes	6.07
Auditing & Legal Fees	0.93
Misc. Office Administration	2.24
Electric	9.33
Water	3.73
General Liability Insurance	6.89
Capital Reserve Contribution	38.89
Total average monthly assessment/unit	$158.32

Chapter 12

BIG TICKET ITEMS
PART I

If your condo community has common area elements such as a clubhouse, pool, miles of sidewalks, pond, tennis courts, or more than twenty buildings, then the board better know its stuff when it comes to construction, financing, and liability exposure. The board should also have a good understanding of its community demographics.

Common area elements require a lot of money for replacement and can't all be replaced at the same time.

Big projects generate a lot of noise and push-back from association segments with self-interest agendas.

All of the aforementioned common area elements require a lot of money for maintenance and replacement. All of them cannot be replaced at one time to satisfy all of the different interest groups in the community. Not everyone swims, walks a dog, plays tennis, or goes to clubhouse events. A non-swimmer may not want to help pay for a new community pool that costs 200,000 dollars. A couch potato may not want to pay for *any* amenities and probably should not have moved into a condo community in the first place.

In one association I managed, it was the president who wasn't into fun in the sun. He thought the community pool (which was used by about forty percent of the membership) was a complete waste of money and proposed filling in the pool with sand and burying it. And so it is with all common elements or amenities in a condo community. Even when it comes to replacing a building roof or sidewalk, you will always hear things like, "Why do I have to pay for their roof?"

Capital Reserve Projects

Ultimately, the association membership will dictate the projects that are acceptable through the ballot box at board elections. If boards waste an association's funds on unnecessary projects, they will eventually be removed by people like me. I know because I've been there and done that.

So how does a condo board play the cards they're dealt in terms of maintaining or replacing the big-ticket items in their community? You really can't just bury them. You will have to manage the big projects as efficiently as your budget allows over periods of several years.

For example, how does an association replace sixty-three building roofs or five miles of sidewalk that were all constructed between 1970 and 1973? They were constructed at much lower prices than today's construction costs, aged similarly, and needed to be replaced at about the same time. That's the hand I was dealt when I entered the condo industry as a board treasurer. I must have been crazy to run as treasurer, because I knew that the capital reserve fund only had $36,000 in it. Previous boards and memberships were negligent in building an adequate reserve fund.

But even if the board has built an adequate reserve fund, that is only half the problem solved. How do you manage such large projects simultaneously? It takes perseverance, patience, tenacity, and board continuity to fight the political headwinds that come with long-term projects. If it's not done right, assessments will rise and residence market values will fall.

Multiple Simultaneous Projects

In the large community where I live, manage, and am on the board, there were simultaneous building, roof, and concrete replacement projects ongoing for a long time. Three to five roofs ($20,000 to $30,000 per roof) and approximately 8,000 square feet of sidewalk ($60,000 to $70,000) are replaced per year. The roof replacement project started in the 1990s and the sidewalk project started in 2003. In addition to these large ongoing projects, the board decided to upgrade a one-acre pond at the community's entrance. The pond project was estimated to cost about 100,000 dollars and would take one year to complete.

So, what's a condo board supposed to do? Generally speaking, the following are needed for a board or manager to deal with multiple, simultaneous big-ticket projects in your community:

- A complete description of the projects
- Duration and completion date of projects
- Estimated cost of projects
- Well defined bidding process for awarding of contracts
- Contractor payment schedules
- Monitoring of progress through time logs, photographs, daily diary, etc.

It's Dirty Work

Construction work cannot be done without some or all of the following, depending on the time of the year: equipment and truck noise, dust and dirt, mud, sidewalk and parking detours, workmen's chatter, and other miscellaneous annoyances and inconveniences.

It's important to ask unit owners to exercise patience and tolerance while construction enhancements are taking place. You know... that time period between "When's mine gonna be done?" and "When are they gonna be outta here?"

The Clubhouse

The clubhouse in any condo community is an important amenity. It can quickly become the focal point of a community. It can be utilized for a variety of events and activities. Sometimes it might be a deal maker or deal breaker if you have or don't have one in your community. A well-managed and preserved clubhouse increases the community's residential unit market values.

Pride in the new clubhouse stimulated a metamorphosis of the social committee.

But such an amenity comes with great responsibility and large expenses. Proper insurances must be in place, and reserve funds have to be established for eventual rejuvenation. The association's operating fund must also budget the annual operating expenses of the clubhouse.

In late 2011, one of my communities decided to remodel its clubhouse. It had one large room with a fireplace, a small kitchen, two small side rooms (infrequently used) and two bathrooms. I described the interior design as "country geriatric." There was no doubt it needed remodeling.

The condo board retained the services of an interior designer. The only thing bigger than her ideas were the words she used to describe them. Nonetheless, it was agreed (for starters) that she would come up with a plan for a new interior design. Her fee for producing a plan was reasonable enough, and in a few weeks she presented her plan. Though interesting, its execution would cost approximately $150,000. This was about $75,000 more than the proposed project budget. She had earned her fee, but did not win the project.

After such an eye-opening experience, the board decided to take a different approach in accomplishing its project goal. With my construction and accounting experience, I convinced the board they could self-manage the project for $75,000 or less. The association maintenance staff (three men) and I (the manager) would do most of the work including demolition, rough framing, drywall, painting, and electrical wiring. The kitchen cabinetry, wet bar, plumbing, and flooring would be subcontracted. The association would purchase new kitchen appliances.

We completed the entire project during the winter months over a three-year period from 2012 to 2014 for a total cost of $75,000 (within budget). There were no disruptions in clubhouse activities since the project was completed in three phases: Phase I, large room and adjacent wet bar; Phase II, entrance foyer and side room; Phase III, kitchen.

As a result of this project, the profitable outside rentals increased substantially as word-of-mouth advertising spread far and wide. Pride in the new clubhouse stimulated a metamorphosis of the social committee, and a variety of new activities and events were held every month. The whole project gave a great lift to the community. Outside, a bocce ball court was added to the pool, tennis court, and shuffleboard area for all to enjoy.

The traditional project route was bypassed, and a more practical path was taken. There is always a better solution when people with good minds and a lot of energy get together. Condo associations with budgets of limited funds have to learn to innovate. If they don't, they will have to learn to do without, raise monthly assessments, or create special assessments to enhance their communities.

The Pool

I have managed two complete pool renovations in my management career. My initial experience began in the spring of 2006. I took on a new community association that had a small kidney-shaped pool and unfinished pool house. This community was being mismanaged by a three-member board that would soon be removed and replaced by a five-member board. The association had minimum capital reserve funds to replace large ticket facilities.

Because of its location in the center of the community, the pool, which was in bad condition, was a diamond in the rough. It could be seen by many of the building units that were at a higher elevation. I envisioned an aqua "gem" during the evening hours, enhanced by underwater pool lighting (which didn't work at the time). But this pool had become a local joke. It was visited more by non-residents who acted as if it were the township pool, than by residents. What the outsider swimmers didn't know was that the pool was infrequently cleaned and hadn't been drained in several years. I convinced the new board to clean it up and make it health-code legal. So the pool was drained, power washed, and outfitted with new underwater lights. We cleaned up the shrubbery around the pool and upgraded the pool bathroom. We also installed a new pool pump. When everything was finally rejuvenated, it reminded me of the resort pool setting in Bermuda where I had spent my honeymoon in 1982.

A few years later when this association had built up its capital reserve fund, we replaced the pool capstones and tile. Then we dry-walled, tiled, and painted the pool house to make it an attractive and functional community facility for pool parties. Within a few years, a pool that had been neglected since the community's inception was rejuvenated, increasing the ambiance and market value of the community. My first major pool upgrade experience was a raving success. It was also a tremendous confidence builder.

Not long after, the largest community that I managed needed improvements to the pool lounging area that surrounded their pool. The community demographic was rapidly getting younger, as approximately twenty-five to thirty units per year were changing ownership. Many younger people and children were attending the pool, and more space became necessary.

The board quickly decided to enlarge the pool area by expanding the perimeter fencing. And since they were at it, they decided to replace the thirty-year-old, beat-up aluminum fence with an aesthetically appealing, earth-toned vinyl fence. At the same time, we removed the four old lamppost streetlights from the pool area and replaced them with twenty-two lantern lights attached to the top of the new fence. The four lamppost streetlights were re-installed in a dimly lit area around the management office parking lot. With the help of the community's in-house maintenance staff, the entire project cost only $10,000. This renovation enabled more frequent and pleasurable evening swim parties and was well-received by all of the residents.

Chapter 13

BIG TICKET ITEMS
PART II

Concrete Considerations

Most communities have common area sidewalks. Their maintenance, repair, and replacement are the responsibility of the association. For the most part, associations delegate this sidewalk supervision to the manager and maintenance crew.

Good condo boards and managers should try to solve problems in the most expeditious and cost efficient way. They don't have to settle for doing it just like everyone else.

When sidewalks are evaluated for replacement, many factors are taken into consideration: condition of sidewalk in relation to all other community sidewalks, necessity of existing sidewalk, drainage issues, winter storm maintenance, ramps versus steps, railings, ambulatory condition of unit's residents, and the contractor's recommendation.

Properly placed concrete can last a long time if it is maintained properly. Nonetheless, it will have to be replaced at some point in time, so eventually it has to be designated and saved for in the association's reserve fund. If your community's sidewalks were completed before municipal construction codes became credible, they may have been placed on earth with little or no stone base under the concrete. This seriously compromises the walks' stability, drainage, and durability. Without a base (four inches recommended), sections can sink as much as two or three inches into the turf. So, if your association is going to replace miles of sidewalk, do it right even if the project has to be spread over more years.

Make sure that whoever does your concrete work has a good "bedside manner" with owners and residents. In other words, be sure the contractors are courteous and respectful during the replacement process when unit owners are being inconvenienced and their safety is being compromised. Temporary ingress and egress accommodations must be made, and some hand-holding may be required. If you don't pay attention to these issues, you're risking a big liability lawsuit. Contractors should be polite and patient—not rough ogres.

The concrete sidewalk replacement process can be more extensive than most condo residents and even board members realize. The basic steps of a complete and safe replacement are as follows:

- ☐ Request bids to do the complete job. Compare bids and check references. Inspect other contractors' work. The low bidder may not be the overall best contractor for your community.
- ☐ Plan project start date, preferably in non-freezing weather.
- ☐ Identify placement of underground utilities.
- ☐ Excavate to remove old sidewalk and simultaneously construct temporary walks for unit access.
- ☐ Provide adequate stone base and drainage under or adjacent to walk.

- [ ] Pour, finish, and seal concrete.
- [ ] Backfill soil to sidewalk and tamp.
- [ ] Plant grass seed and restore disturbed landscape.

Each sidewalk installation has its own character. Boards and contractors will need to be able to adapt to changing circumstances and landscapes. Perhaps ramps would be better than steps. Wider walks may be necessary. Some sidewalks could be eliminated. Any sidewalk can be modified to meet changing landscapes and demographics.

From the Manager's Desk: Hard Decisions

Most of Glencreek is now more than thirty-five years old. The sidewalks and landscaping improvements are evidence that Glencreek is a "work in progress" which will never be done. But things can always be improved upon, and the board is committed to keeping the community a "gold standard" of condos in Lancaster County.

There are approximately five miles of sidewalks in Glencreek. Replacing them would be a financially draining project. It would have to be done over several years as the capital reserve fund would also have to pay for roofs, paving, and other big ticket projects. The executive board decided to move forward, so in 2003 we started replacing the feeder sidewalks leaving the 2.4 miles of perimeter walks for the second phase of sidewalk replacement. The replacement of feeder sidewalks is approximately sixty-five percent complete. By the end of 2017, they will be substantially complete at ninety percent. The remaining ten percent are short feeder walks in some two-story building sections that will be done in conjunction with the perimeter sidewalk replacement.

In the end, the feeder sidewalk replacement project will have taken fifteen years. Folks, that's a result of determination, perseverance, and fiduciary responsibility of several boards, management, and one great concrete contractor. That's the good news!

The bad news is that the 2.4 miles of perimeter walks will have to be replaced at an approximate cost of $500,000. Keep in mind that the rejuvenation of Glencreek will be never-ending. There will always be roofs, paving, gutters, downspouts, patios, fences, plumbing, and siding replacements ongoing.

The Pond

In my community's township, I achieved notoriety as "that pond guy." The association's pond was next to a heavily traveled highway at a traffic light intersection. Passersby saw me slugging it out with the pond features every day for a year. When it was completed, the board acknowledged my Herculean effort by naming the pond "Leo's Pond." The pond project outline was as follows:

☐ Obtain bid, although there was only one pond contractor in the area who could manage the project
☐ Obtain project blueprint from contractors

- ☐ Negotiate contract price
- ☐ Acquire 200 tons of large boulders
- ☐ Drain pond as necessary
- ☐ Remove and relocate expensive koi fish population
- ☐ Pump thirty years of accumulated non-toxic sludge from pond (approximately 300 cubic yards)
- ☐ Remove old, leaking pond liner
- ☐ Reshape interior pond contour to new configuration
- ☐ Install new fill pipe plumbing and new liner
- ☐ Partially fill pond to approximate three-foot depth
- ☐ Re-introduce koi fish population
- ☐ Install two new illuminated fountains
- ☐ Install new community entrance signage
- ☐ Landscape perimeter of pond

Yikes! Now that's a big project. I can truthfully say that the effectiveness of this outline was better understood after the project than at its inception. About three months into the project—shockingly and to everyone's surprise—I fired the pond-scape contractor for lack of performance. The remaining two-thirds of the project was completed by me and my go-to guy, the association's concrete contractor. Why? Because he had the equipment to move and install the large boulders, some of which weighed two tons.

The progress and completion of my once-in-a-lifetime pond project is detailed in the following pages. It was hard work, even scary at times. It required perseverance and a daring spirit. I loved it and hated it—sometimes in the same day. Eventually, I was very proud of it. I'm too old to do it again (hands-on, that is), but you can call me if you need some advice.

New Pond Liner Installation

From the Manager's Desk: Pond Repair

The large pond on the north side of Glencreek Drive needs some extensive repairs. Due to increased water intake from commercial development north of Glencreek, the banks of the pond have been subject to accelerated erosion. This erosion has to be stopped and earth has to be replaced. Also, due to wear and tear and pond overfilling, the thirty-year-old pond liner leaks and should be replaced. This will by no means be an easy project.

It is complicated by the fact that there is a structural and environmental relationship between our large pond and the small pond across Glencreek Drive that is owned by our new neighbors. At this time, the executive board is also planning to enhance the community's main entrance signage. Once the scope of this project is determined and a strategic engineering plan (including pond landscaping and signage) is drawn up, the work will proceed.

As always, Glencreek management will plan and shop this project carefully so it can be accomplished in the most cost-efficient manner. For example, I was able to secure approximately $8,000 worth of large boulders from our neighbors' construction project for the cost of three dump truck deliveries—a total of $150—no charge for boulders. The Glencreek maintenance staff will be made available to the project contractor to defer some of the cost.

Again, I must stress that this project has become a priority. It won't be long before our pond will be eroding the adjacent state road right-of-way and then PennDOT will be in my office telling me what we can and cannot do.

Leo Relocating Koi to Holding Tank

From the Manager's Desk: In Need of Drought

In the July issue of the Glencreek newsletter I gave a preview of the pond project. Due to many questions, concerns, and critiques of the project to date, I thought an update would be appropriate.

I forewarned in my preview that this project would be a new experience for me, and three weeks into the project, I can tell you it is not progressing as quickly as I thought, mainly due to the sludge on top of the old liner in the bottom of the pond. The original estimate of sludge tonnage, when under water, was 100 tons which would have taken about two days to remove. The actual amount of sludge removed was 325 tons! This took about five days to remove as the weather permitted. A couple of equipment break-downs have added to the slow progress.

As I am writing this article, the pond contractor is preparing to cut a shelf around the pond to install the edging of the liner. Not unexpectedly, water had to be pumped out of the pond area for the seventh time, due to last night's rain.

If residents wish to view the work in progress, please do so from outside the caution tape and without questioning or socializing with the construction workers. Crawling under the caution barriers to get a better look from the rocks is probably not a good idea from an OSHA and insurance point of view.

To date, we have already made some changes which will lead to better control of storm water from our northern neighbors and a cleaner-looking pond. In the meantime—pray for no rain.

The Levee

For years I managed and was a board member of a community that had a natural storm water swale that bisected an area of the landscape. It was about a quarter of a mile long and was a scenic feature of the community. When it overflowed, however, it was scary.

Usually people don't care where water flows, as long as it passes their property without harm or property damage. Once it passes, it becomes someone else's problem. The community was downstream and immediately adjacent to a state-owned property. For many years, the state's natural storm water swale was not troublesome. With modern day suburban sprawl upstream (more roofs, more pavement, more streets, and parking lots), the storm water runoff created flooding conditions in my condo community.

Compounding the problem was the fact that the adjacent state property expanded its tourist parking lot. All of the extra water coming down from the northern development and the state's parking lot emptied into a large, unimproved concrete culvert pipe that passed under the road and into a natural swale that passed through the state's farm field into our condo community's property. Over time the increased water runoff deposited silt, assorted plant debris, and trash into the swale as it passed through the state's property.

Consequently, the swale clogged up, flattened out, and caused flooding of the field. A small pond would form after a heavy rainstorm. What was once a farm field morphed into a wetlands area. The ducks, geese, herons, and other aquatic creatures noticed. Though very interesting to me as an outdoorsman, it created a big problem for me to solve.

When the field reached its holding limit, the overflow flooded the association's property boundary over a one hundred foot long area. The flooding threatened nearby units, including my unit. On several occasions when this flooding occurred, I invited the township officials to visit the site and witness the problem at its worst. What was their reaction and response? With a shrug of shoulders, they said, "The township storm water engineering plan was designed to handle the water." To which I responded, "My eyes are telling me that the plan isn't working." Well, my pleas for improvements fell on deaf ears, but eventually something did change. Unfortunately, the change came through a lot of hard work by me.

I'm not proposing or advocating that all condo associations tackle such a project in such a hands-on manner.

To clean up this mess, all that was necessary was for the landowner (the state of Pennsylvania) to assume the responsibility for dredging its portion of the drainage swale that passed through its property. Then the storm water could, once again, flow unimpeded. I pleaded for such a remedy several times to the state's property manager but he wasn't very responsive to the additional workload. I think he was near retirement. But really, who wants to deal with the state in any capacity? So, as always, I decided to go it alone, but only after my solution was approved by the board.

Early one spring when I began the annual community sidewalk replacement project, I instructed the concrete contractor to deposit the excavated material in the flood area zone. He was instructed to build a four foot high by twelve foot wide pile of stone and dirt for 100 feet along the association's property where the water flooded. This was to be the backbone of the levee that would hold back the floodwater and funnel it into the natural swale. The levee was then back-filled with gravel and dirt. By autumn, the levee was almost complete, needing only topsoil and seeding. When the snow began to fly, the community levee had nice grass and was complete.

There was no flooding that winter. The levee has been tested many times since and has worked perfectly. The "icing on the cake" was that the project was completed at minimal expense to the association. My concrete guy did all of the heavy machine work with his backhoe, and I did all of the hand work on my management time. Shoveling, raking, grading, tamping, and seeding became my daily exercise. Once again my dad's lessons to stay strong and healthy paid big dividends. I had tackled this project in my 60th year and physically, it was no big deal.

I'm not proposing or advocating that all condo associations tackle such a project in such a hands-on manner. The message is this: where there is a will, there is a way. Good condo boards and managers should try to solve problems in the most expeditious and cost efficient way. They don't have to settle for doing it just like everyone else. My experience has taught me that there are usually non-traditional ways to solve problems. That is how I made my mark in the condo industry. All it took was knowledge, strength, and persever-ance. Certainly, there is no monopoly on such traits.

Projects Completed

At the risk of being redundant, in my experience an on-site management staff and maintenance department is the best way to take care of a condo community. Unfortunately, in order to maximize residential acreage and sales, condo project devel-opers rarely provide an on-site management and maintenance facility. Developers are rarely concerned about the community's future management and maintenance needs. When they're out—they're out!

Over the years with the assistance of my maintenance staff, I have completed many large projects. These are some of the projects that we completed in a self-managed condo community over a ten-year period. An outside management company would have had a difficult time achieving such success at the lowest possible cost.

- ☐ New maintenance yard fence with lighting
- ☐ Six new maintenance garage doors
- ☐ Pond rejuvenation with new liner and fountains
- ☐ New entrance signage
- ☐ Construction of Veterans Memorial Patio and flagpole
- ☐ Resurfacing of tennis courts
- ☐ Retaining wall adjacent to pool bathrooms
- ☐ Remodeling of pool bathrooms
- ☐ Remodeling of management offices and porch
- ☐ Remodeling of pump house
- ☐ Remodeling of clubhouse
- ☐ Regrading of Glencreek swale and levee construction
- ☐ New community benches
- ☐ Forty-nine new building roofs
- ☐ Complete painting of exterior clubhouse
- ☐ Sixty thousand square feet of sidewalk replacement
- ☐ More than two hundred new trees planted
- ☐ Enlargement of the pool area with new pool fence and lighting
- ☐ Installation of TV satellite dishes
- ☐ Achievement of "Gold Star Community" recognition by CAI

Chapter 14

KEEPING IT CLASSY

Curb Appeal

When a potential buyer drives into your condo community for the first time there has to be something that quickly makes a positive impression. How can your association create some immediate curb appeal? Pay attention to the following:

- ☐ Install a grand main entrance with professional signage, lighting, and landscaping.
- ☐ Make sure the main streets through community are paved, sealed, and pothole free.
- ☐ Install effective but reserved street and parking area lighting , with lights shining downward.
- ☐ Have curbside grass mowed and clippings picked up.
- ☐ Have the sidewalks along the main streets edged neatly.
- ☐ Keep curbside trees and plants trimmed and thinned of dead growth.
- ☐ Make sure that some color from trees, shrubs, and plants is visible.
- ☐ If possible, keep vehicles off the streets and in parking lots or garages.
- ☐ Ensure that building unit numbers are visible from the streets.

☐ In winter, keep the streets and parking lots reasonably cleaned up.

☐ Use appropriate and adequate signage (speed, enter, exit, one-way, visitor parking, etc.). Too much signage is too busy and unattractive.

☐ Properly identify and present the community's best amenity (clubhouse, pool, walking paths, tennis courts etc.).

☐ Have some benches throughout the community for walker's rest stops.

☐ Don't allow junk to accumulate outside building units and no Christmas décor in April.

You get the idea. No condo community is expected to display all of the curb appeal facets listed above, but the more, the better. Remember that there's a certain amount of truth to the saying, "You get what you pay for." A community with all of the above amenities is going to have higher monthly assessments, but there has to be enough curb appeal to the get the prospective buyers out of their cars to take a closer look or ask their realtor some questions.

Pool Area

Many years ago I attended a seminar on the most common legal challenges to condo associations. The speaker, a Philadelphia attorney, said that the Three P's—Pets, Pools, and Parking—cause the most trouble in condo communities. [See Chapter 18 for Vehicular Challenges and Chapter 20 for Pet Peeves.]

Though I have never experienced any legal conflicts regarding community pools, they can be an expensive amenity if you don't know what you're doing. At a minimum, they will give a board or manager a lot of headaches.

My first grand headache experience with a condo pool was on the morning of July 3, 2004. The July 4th weekend was imminent and the pool pump conked out. It had to be replaced within twenty-four hours. I was not in a very good bargaining position for obtaining a new pump or a contractor to install it. The pump came from a couple states away and arrived on the morning of July 4.

Guests Lining Up for Annual Pool Party

Luckily, I had a good relationship with my plumbing contractor. He was willing to work with our association's maintenance personnel to get the new pump installed in time for the holiday weekend. The timing of this unfortunate circumstance increased the replacement cost, but it was tolerable. The consequences of closing the pool on July 4th weekend would have been intolerable.

What did I learn from this experience? I learned to always have a backup pump, and that when it comes to pools, preventative maintenance is a must. Because of liability exposure, the cleanliness and safety of the pool are top priorities. The health of pool attendees cannot be compromised. This is where the liability exposure lies. A pool must be clean, safe, and secure. Pool attendance policy and pool etiquette are secondary issues.

Pool Safety and Etiquette

Most condo pools are not required to have lifeguards. Some have lifeguards even if they're not required. It's an accommodation for the safety and convenience of the attendees. A community association owes a duty of reasonable care to every person who enters a pool area.

Does the presence of a lifeguard really limit the association's exposure? If a lifeguard is negligent in overseeing the pool area, doesn't that neglect expose the association if there is a tragic event? A responsible lifeguard may give an association a reasonable defense, but could still cause the association to incur legal costs. There is no easy solution to the pool oversight dilemma. Boards and managers must simply do their best, using common sense as a guide.

Newsletter articles would not be necessary if all pool attending residents acted with respect. The issue at hand will likely be addressed many times over the years without any consistent success.

At the beginning of the pool season, management and maintenance arrange the pool tables, chairs, and loungers with some planning and purpose. This furniture arrangement is based on experience. It's done for a variety of reasons including neatness, socialization, to get the sun's rays more directly, or for more privacy. That's okay—no problem yet.

The problem begins when the furniture has been rearranged but is not moved back to its original placement. As the person who handled this furniture the most, I definitely learned all the subtleties after ten years of pool management. Inconsiderate pool etiquette leads to a lot of extra labor and expense. Keeping the pool area neat and classy, as well as safe, should be a job for everyone to share. Ask residents to return the furniture to its original placement.

From the Manager's Desk: Times Are Changing

Glencreek Management has noticed a demographic change taking place in the community since 2005. During the past several years, over one hundred units have changed ownership. One of the community areas where this demographic shift is noticeable is in the pool. Younger children are attending the pool, because there are younger parents and grandparents who have purchased units. Add in the great-grandchildren and you've got a pool playground.

As a result of this demographic phenomenon, the quiet atmosphere of the pool, which older residents have become accustomed to, is being challenged by the noise and activity of youth. With more young children and toddlers accessing the pool, new safety and health concerns have been expressed to management and lifeguards.

We are paying close attention to this increased activity at the pool and will be consulting with the executive board about tweaking the pool policy to accommodate the changing demographics, so that all pool attendees can enjoy themselves.

Chapter 15

LANDSCAPING

THE GRASS IS ALWAYS GREENER . . .

Landscape management, especially in large acreage communities, requires a big-picture approach. It's not just about one small patch of grass or one tree limb. It's about 400 lawns and 1,000 trees. Though the grass and trees are jointly owned by the association members, they are managed by the board. It's a big responsibility. The landscaping contract is usually the largest maintenance expense item in the annual budget. It cannot be taken lightly.

Although I am neither a tree hugger nor a tree mugger, sometimes I have gone out on a limb to accommodate divergent views on tree management.

Tree management alone in a mature, landscaped community is a difficult, expensive, and thankless job. What about the grass? Well, it's too short to hug unless you lie on it. But a community can have just as much trouble with grass as it has with trees. It's cut too short or too tall; it's too thick or too thin; the new grass is a different color than the old grass.

And my favorite of all time, "When they mow the grass, why can't they get it to all lean in the same direction?"

A lot of residents sit by the window, watch, and dream up this stuff. They see everything. I knew one busybody who duct-taped an old car rear view mirror on her computer monitor so she could see out of the window behind her while she sat at the computer. She wouldn't miss anything. Can you imagine the scrutiny that the landscape contractor was subject to? "The mowers make too much noise. Can't they install mufflers?" or "Why do they have to go forty miles per hour?" "Why do mowers have to go in circles around the trees?" Okay, you get the picture.

Team Effort

When you move into a condo community, leave the "I's" at the front gate and starting thinking "we."

When it comes to landscaping, the move from a private detached home setting to a condo community can cause culture shock for new residents. The grass, shrubbery, and trees adjacent to a unit or building are not *privately* owned—just *partly* owned. We've all heard the phrase "There is no I in team." Well, there are two "I's" in condominium, but in order to get along with their neighbors, managers, and boards, all unit owners need to become team players. When you move into a condo community, leave the "I's" at the front gate and starting thinking "We."

The landscaping in a condominium community is usually the property of the condo association unless it's growing inside a building unit. If the condo association allows unit owners to plant a tree or shrub in the common area, it then belongs to the association. But a simple generous act can set a dangerous precedent in a condo community. If the board allows one unit owner to do something, all unit owners should be allowed to do it. And then you end up with too many trees. Such is the nature of the "all for one—one for all" philosophy of the condo association. That's why it's important to get everyone on the same team.

Landscape Bids

When I managed a large community with thirty-three acres to mow and over 1,200 trees to manage, I put the landscaping contract out for bid every three years. Even though I was satisfied with the current landscape contractor, the large cost of the contract necessitated a competitive "check and balance."

When I received the bids for this community, the price range was always bothersome. From experience, I knew that a reasonable bid was in the $150,000 range. Over the years, I received bids as low as $60,000 and as high as $477,000.

The $60,000 bid was submitted by an Amish contractor. When I didn't vote to accept this ridiculously low bid, a Jewish board member accused me, Leo Rosenberger (of German descent), of discriminating against the Amish (of German descent). In the board member's defense, I should note that I had in fact made a wisecrack about allowing mules to pull the mowers in the community. Sometimes, my mom's Irish wit gets me in trouble.

I'm not sure what the high bidder was thinking. Perhaps he never got out of his pickup when inspecting the community. It happens.

Tree Management

When trees and shrubs are planted in newly constructed condo communities there is often not much forethought given to the tree selection process. And guess what? Twenty or thirty years later there are a lot of mature trees in places they shouldn't be.

Having been raised a hunter and fisherman in the rural Catskill Mountain region of New York, I deeply appreciate the aesthetic beauty and ecological value of trees. I have always done my best for the benefit of all trees under my management. Since becoming a community association manager in 2003, I have instigated the planting of about two hundred trees. Although I am neither a tree hugger nor a tree mugger, sometimes I have gone out on a limb to accommodate divergent views on tree management.

There are different philosophies about tree management— from letting nature take its course to spending money on fertilizer, spraying, and pruning. Because associations work within limited budgets, they should likely take a middle-of-the-road approach to tree management, doing what is necessary to keep tree landscaping mature and attractive.

Some residents love the trees, some hate the trees, and some don't care. Managers really don't know where some people stand on a particular tree until it becomes a nuisance or danger to adjacent residents. Mention the phrases "trim it" or "cut it down" and the opinions change and the negotiations begin.

At one point, I completed a tree census of a community I managed. One thing was for sure—it had a lot of trees! Hardwood, evergreen, old, young, healthy, diseased, nutty, fruity, messy, and colorful. Some trees were there before the oldest residents were born, before the community existed. Many were planted in the past forty years.

However, when trees are in an environment that's not suitable to their needs, or if they're confined to small spaces where their roots and branches are a nuisance or cause damage, then tree management can be challenging.

Some trees will have varying degrees of stress due to a lack of ecological symbiosis. A minority eke out a miserable existence (pin oaks). Nutty trees, though loved by some (squirrels), are a nuisance to management and maintenance. Oak trees that are too close to sidewalks and parking lots drop marble-like acorns that people can slip on. Fruity trees, such as crab apples, make sticky messes on sidewalks and cars. They have beautiful spring blossoms and spectacular red fall apples, but mowers, people, and cars crush the apples into a slippery mash. Though beautiful in autumn, maples and other leafy trees (if planted upwind and too close to the buildings) will clog rain gutters and downspouts for a few months. Pine trees drop sticky sap on cars—if planted too near the parking lots—and in gutters of units that are too close. Lastly, the locust drops an overripe banana-like pod that sticks to the pavement and has to be shoveled away, if not blown away on a frequent basis.

Except for the very messy locust trees, I did not cut down healthy trees. Once in a great while a nuisance tree had to be cut down to size with a chainsaw. Generally speaking, trees that we removed had been damaged by weather or disease.

On only one occasion did a tree cry before its demise (a weeping willow).

Tree Removal

Trimming a bothersome tree is always the first line of defense. Mature trees are very expensive to take down and dispose of. Therefore, if there is no other good reason to take a tree down, the cost of removal alone would allow its survival.

No one likes to see a big old tree come down. But it's the circle of plant life, nothing more, nothing less.

In one community that I managed there was a row of locust trees through a parking lot. One of the mature locust's roots eventually strangled a water main and broke it, causing major problems for half the community. Of course, it had to happen in late autumn on a cold, rainy night. Contractors were contacted to excavate a four-foot deep hole to find the break. Once they found it, they had to cut the roots away from the pipe prior to the installation of a connector sleeve. The hard-working young men did not have a chainsaw to do the work, so I got mine. There I was, in a muddy hole at two in the morning, cutting the roots of the locust tree from the pipe. Within a week after this incident, I called in my tree guy to remove all three of the locust trees growing over the rest of the main water line. Unsurprisingly, I incurred the wrath of the tree huggers in the community.

It is much more difficult to remove a tree than to plant one, and the decision to remove a tree should not be taken lightly. When safety is a concern it's an easier decision to make.

To properly and safely remove a tree from the landscape requires the following process:

1. Arrange for tree felling by a qualified contractor.
2. Remove tree debris.

3. Alert the One-Call system to mark stump area for underground utilities.
4. Arrange for stump removal by contractor.
5. Grade ex-stump area to prepare for seeding.
6. Add topsoil to affected area.
7. Plant grass seed.
8. Cover seeded area with straw.
9. Water area if necessary.
10. Mow by hand until grass takes hold.

No one likes to see a big old tree come down. But it's the circle of plant life, nothing more, nothing less.

Leo on the Stump

Chapter 16

UTILITIES

NOW YOU SEE 'EM, NOW YOU DON'T

Nothing has less curb appeal than a building with all kinds of pipes, wires, and satellite dishes attached to it. Hide your utilities whenever possible to increase the aesthetic appeal and market value of your community. Communities simply look better when there is less paraphernalia attached to buildings or installed in the landscape.

The only thing uglier than a satellite dish is a lot of dishes in close proximity to each other.

Cost Factors

Utility expense in a condo community is one of the board's lesser concerns. Small communities will have small budgets for common utilities. Communities that have additional facilities or amenities will incur greater expense and need monitoring. For instance, pools generate high electric and water bills. Tennis courts may require evening lighting and, of course, a clubhouse will generate all types of extra utility expense. Many communities have street lamp lighting. Simply use the most efficient bulbs for this kind of lighting. Sometimes, a more expensive bulb (LED) produces the most effective lighting over the long term.

Safety Factors

If an association uses natural gas for heating, close monitoring by management is necessary. In today's economy, gas-fired hot air systems are the most cost-efficient heating utility. Unit utilities are typically the responsibility of unit owners. But when gas lines are involved, association management or maintenance has to play a more active role in assuring the safety of all residents in a building. Gas and an older, more forgetful demographic is a dangerous mixture. On more than one occasion, I have discovered residents using a gas range as an additional heat source. Some even bring their summer gas grills inside their units for additional heat.

When construction work has to be completed on under-ground utilities (especially gas), the one-call system to iden-tify all utilities in the work zone must be utilized. This safety measure incurs minimum expense but offers maximum safety precaution.

Lastly, make sure all telephone, electric, TV, and Internet cables are covered by sufficient depth of topsoil/mulch to avoid being cut by mowers, tillers, and edgers.

Plumbing: Whose Pipe Is It?

Water or sewer plumbing problems in a condo community are usually about leaks, clogs, and boundaries. Whatever the problem, it can be fixed, but the repair cost may or may not be expensive. Controversy arises when it's time to pay the bill. Whose responsibility is it, the association's or the unit owner's? Not unlike every other condo solution, this is not as easy to ascertain as it may first appear.

The plumbing boundaries (who's responsible for what) are described in great detail in the condo declaration's "plots and plans" section. But who reads the declaration or still has it in mind since the purchase ten years ago? The only time it's important enough to read is when the unit owner is billed for plumbing work that he doesn't think he should have to pay. Even after reading, the plumbing-challenged mind can find the details difficult to understand. It's like trying to understand "legalese."

Most condo owners think their repair responsibilities and related costs end on the other side of the paint on their interior walls. This is generally true. However, with water and sewer pipes, there are condo nuances. Usually each condo building has a common main water pipe that supplies the entire building. Repairs to that pipe are usually the responsibility of the association. The cost of repair is funded by community assessments. In other words, it's "all for one—and one for all." The feeder line/pipe that branches off the common area pipe (main line) and supplies an individual unit, however, can be the unit owner's responsibility in many associations. Make sure that unit owners have a clear understanding of this issue. The confusion lies in the fact that, although the unit's individual feeder pipe is outside the wall in what is generally considered the common area, it may still be the unit owner's responsibility. It's an exception.

Most condo owners think their repair responsibilities end on the other side of the paint on their interior walls.

Like water pipe plumbing, there is also a main or common area sewer pipe that carries waste from the building. Each condo unit has its own individual piping that drains bathroom and kitchen waste into the main line that exits the building. The feeder lines may be 1.5" in diameter and the main line 4" in diameter.

It's surprising what people will try to dispose of in a kitchen sink or toilet. Just because Seinfeld's neighbor,

Cosmo Kramer, installed a garbage disposer in his bathroom shower so he could make salads while bathing, doesn't mean it works. It's a TV show, folks! Think it can't happen? Then how do you explain twenty-seven banana peels or an undamaged lemon clogging a sewer line? Either someone's intestines are not doing their job or someone is crazy. Or it's plumbing sabotage. One unit resident did eventually confess to making banana bread. The lemon incident is still an open case. Nonetheless, the occupants of the units where the fruit disposals took place got the bill for unclogging the sewer line. No lawyers were necessary.

Many condo associations bear the cost to unclog main sewer lines when the cause of the clog is more reasonable (or less absurd). But specific identification of a negligent action by a condo resident is justification for billing the guilty party. Personally, I'd rather do jail time before I'd pay an assessment to share the cost of such idiocy.

Satellite Dishes

There is nothing attractive about a satellite dish. The only thing uglier than a satellite dish is a lot of dishes in close proximity to each other on buildings and landscape. That's why it's best that dishes be hidden as much as possible in a condo community. This is easier said than done. Mature tree growth and building location can interfere or prevent access to the satellite in the sky. Since condo associations control the common areas in their communities, they are offered some latitude by the FCC (Federal Communications Commission) as to where dishes can be installed on buildings and in landscape (roofs, walls, and shrub beds).

TV satellite dishes should not be installed on roofs or building walls unless there is no other alternative. Anytime a roof or building is penetrated by an outside contractor, there is exposure to future problems, such as leaks or insect and rodent infestation. The penetration of a roof is never a good idea for any reason. If you don't have to do it—then don't. Holes in roofs usually lead to problems which increase maintenance time and expense.

From the Manager's Desk: It Ain't Your Roof

At Glencreek, there are no dishes on shingled ranch-style buildings. Also, dishes are not allowed to be installed on outside walls. Dishes are allowed in ranch-style building patios and planting beds, but only after approval by the association manager or governing board. Installation of dishes is allowed on two-story building flat roofs (only), but in such a manner that does not require roof penetration. They can be securely placed on rubber pads, and the accompanying wires can be run into the building in an aesthetically acceptable way. Again, only with prior management approval.

After almost two years of investigation, interrogation, deliberation, consideration, and frustration, Glencreek had its first rooftop satellite dish installation. It is atop building 300-307 in case you haven't noticed. You shouldn't notice it, since that was part of the plan.

The satellite dish is attached to a hard rubber pad and simply sits atop the flat portion on the east end of the building. No roof mount penetration was necessary. The cable runs inconspicuously off the roof into the housing unit.

At Glencreek, we aim to please, while operating within architectural, cost efficient, and visually acceptable constraints. Please direct satellite installation inquiries to the management office.

- ☐ The mounting of satellite dishes on Glencreek buildings must be approved in advance by Glencreek management.
- ☐ Don't believe satellite dish sales people or technicians who say they got approval from the office to

mount a dish. You must get approval directly from the management and not from the dish installers.

☐ The mounting of a dish cannot take place on a Saturday or Sunday. Technicians must check in at the office Monday through Friday 8-4:30 p.m.

☐ According to the FCC, community associations are given wide latitude in determining where dishes are installed on buildings or landscapes.

You must remember that you are part of an association and part of an association building—not a single-family detached residence. Adherence to association policy is management's expectation. If you hear neighbors talking about dishes or see an installation in progress, please tell them about the requirements and/or notify the office.

Trash Removal

When I was a young lad my dad once said, "If you're gonna be a ditch digger, then be the best damn ditch digger that you can be." He always preached that you should take pride in your work and do the best you can. And so it should be with trash haulers. Working a trash route is hard, filthy, stinky work. It's stereotypically degrading. Granted, you don't have to have a high GPA to pick up trash. But you should understand (especially if you have had the contract for five years) that if there are 100 units in a condominium community, then it follows that there should be 100 pickups. There shouldn't be mistakes or excuses. Once in awhile, maybe.

Trash hauling contracts should be bid out at least every three years. Just like trash, trash-hauling bids can be all over the place. The haulers may not have high GPAs but they're smart enough to know their hauling costs, including dumping fees and the actual pick-up process. Because of its simple nature, the quality of service should be the same for all bidders. Consequently, winning bids should be based on price. Just ask for some client references and make sure the winning bidder provides a certificate of insurance.

Whenever I hired a new trash hauler, I rode and worked the truck on random occasions to get a feel for the route's demands. It was the way I checked on the efficiency of their pickup system and is another example of my instinctive hands-on approach to management.

My best trash-hauling story happened shortly after I replaced a nationally known trash hauler with a local hauler. The national hauler was hired by the manager who preceded me, so the contract was already in place and had a penalty clause if canceled before expiration. The annual contract was for $36,000 dollars, with a one-month cancellation fee of $3,000 dollars. I found a hauler who would give me a three-year contract at $24,000 dollars per year. That's a $12,000 dollar savings per year—$36,000 over three years.

Believe it or not, a unit owner stood up at the annual open board meeting (when I was up for re-election) and clearly stated, "Mr. Rosenberger, I heard that you paid a $3,000 penalty fee just so you could save $12,000 on the trash contract." She was aghast and scanned the audience for approval of her discovery. I responded by saying, "I saved the association $12,000 a year for the next three years for a total savings of $36,000." While the audience politely chuckled, this lady still didn't get it. Twelve years later and I still don't think she got it.

My dad once said, "If you're gonna be a ditch digger, then be the best damn ditch digger that you can be."

But that's not the end of the story. About three months after this woman's attempt to embarrass me with her misguided "gotcha" moment, the association received a letter from the national trash hauler whose contract I canceled. Inside the envelope was a check for $3,000. The letter said, "Dear Mr. Rosenberger, In reviewing our files, we noticed that your association overpaid its 2004 annual contract in the amount of $3,000. Thank you for your service, and we look forward to bidding on your trash hauling in the future."

Someone in that accounting department mistakenly interpreted my penalty fee for a contract overpayment and refunded the overage. The total savings achieved over the three-year contract was $36,000 rather than $33,000. And the trash service was satisfactory.

From the Manager's Desk: Trash Talkin'

Recently, management had the dilapidated wooden maintenance yard fence demolished and replaced with a new vinyl fence with locking gates. The new fence was considered necessary for aesthetic as well as privacy reasons. The maintenance yard inside the fence is used for the storage of construction and landscaping materials. It's also where the maintenance staff members park their vehicles and receive maintenance supply deliveries. It's where equipment is temporarily stored and repaired. For all of the aforementioned reasons Glencreek maintenance likes to keep this area as free of unnecessary debris and traffic as possible.

Problematically speaking, Glencreek's two trash dumpsters are inside the maintenance yard fence. The dumpsters and this area are supposed to be for the exclusive use of Glencreek maintenance. However, in the past and from time-to-time, Glencreek has allowed residents to dispose of their extra trash items in these dumpsters and the yard. Not surprisingly this "from time-to-time" allowance has escalated to unacceptable and out-of-control dumping. Open yard gates in the evening and on weekends have led to indiscriminate and nuisance dumping. Consequently, Glencreek maintenance staff and trash disposal contractors are spending too much time and money cleaning up messes, especially on Monday mornings.

For example, the removal of large appliances and hazardous waste materials (unused paint) are to be coordinated between unit owners and the trash contractor. Unit owners are financially responsible for the removal of such items. They are not to be dumped in the Glencreek maintenance yard where their removal becomes an association expense and a maintenance nuisance. Also, because of Glencreek's generous open gate policy, residents' indiscriminate dumping habits have exposed the association to an insurance liability issue.

Therefore, after lengthy deliberation and review, Glencreek management will prevent evening and weekend access to the maintenance yard and dumpsters. Management realizes that there will be infrequent special requests for dumpster access and will accommodate or refuse such on a case-by-case basis.

Chapter 17

THE WEATHER OUTSIDE IS FRIGHTFUL

Your community's location geographically will dictate the required storm knowledge and procedures necessary to protect both physical property and residents. In the northeast United States, snow management is the overwhelming storm priority. In the mid-Atlantic region there is some snow, but hurricanes and flooding can be the top priority. Tornado alley is the concern of the Central and

When it comes to snow removal in a condo community, not all residents can be first to get service. Satisfactory cleanup requires time and patience by both maintenance and residents.

Midwest United States, while earthquakes, droughts, and mudslides are problems of the West Coast. Whatever the climate in your region of the country, condominium associations are expected to have the manpower, equipment, and knowledge to deal with storm management. It can have life or death consequences.

Growing up in New York's Catskill Mountains, I experienced all kinds of snow and ice removal. My dad was responsible for the local and county highways and drove a big snowplow truck. Though he cleared the main route that went past our family's general store and gas station, his ethics would not allow him to swing the taxpayers' plow through our store parking lot and gas station area. That was my shoveling responsibility, night or day, or both. I shoveled tons of snow between the ages of six and eighteen, right up until I was relieved of my duties by college attendance. The strong back that was built in those early years continues to serve me well—even at age sixty-six.

Snow and Ice Removal

I am always optimistic about the snow budget when the community gets through November and December with minimal expense, but snow and ice removal can be very tricky. Many factors can come into play, including the timing of the storm, (day, night, or both), depth of precipitation, wind and temperature conditions, duration of the storm, association members' compliance with storm parking procedures, the health condition of the maintenance crew, status of equipment, and the "unexpected." Any of these factors can bust a budget.

If the snow and ice removal in a condo community is done by outside contractors, then the only thing the board or manager has to do is make sure it's done right. Some board members may have ice and snow removal experience, but in most cases, they won't know how to deal with large snowstorms. And the average home-driveway shoveler likely won't understand the complexities, either. What does it take for a crew to deal with large-scale snow or ice removal?

- ☐ High energy
- ☐ Strong backs
- ☐ Weather knowledge and intuition
- ☐ Equipment experience
- ☐ Low sleep requirement
- ☐ Perseverance
- ☐ Safety consciousness
- ☐ Public relations competence

Even if your snow crew has the aforementioned skills, it is difficult to meet the high expectations of helpless snowstorm victims. In condo communities, additional factors include, but are not limited to: the average age of community residents (older is more demanding), the number of parking spaces, the miles of sidewalk and number of steps, provisions for emergency accommodation, and employment status of the community's residents (whether they need to get to work or are retired).

When it comes to snow removal in a condo community, not all residents can be first to get service. Satisfactory cleanup requires time and patience by both maintenance and residents. Prior to the winter season, the board should educate community residents about snowstorm policies and procedures. It's especially important to remind the elderly of safety precautions, as well. For example, remind residents not to go outside unless it is an emergency. I've seen many situations in which elderly residents broke arms, legs, or hips because they felt they just had to get outside and clean off their car windshields. Most snowstorm experience is learned the hard way—through pain or expense. Some people learn it; some don't.

> Winter weather's dangers are worth knowing,
> Especially when you're walking outside,
> Consider not going
> When it's icy or snowing,
> Unless you prefer an ambulance ride.

Winter Storm Procedures

Maintenance staff will need to do its very best with snow removal, but the cooperative efforts of all the residents will certainly help get the job done faster and more smoothly. The following are reminders I have used to let residents know what is expected of them.

- ☐ Pick up any mats or delivered newspapers at your entrance when snow is threatening. Both can damage snow blowers if they get sucked up.
- ☐ Ice melt products work while temperatures are above freezing. Whatever melts and doesn't run off will refreeze until cleared. Only approved ice melt products can be used on new concrete sidewalks. Call maintenance with any questions regarding this issue.
- ☐ Allow reasonable time for maintenance to clear snow from sidewalks leading from parking lots to units. Sidewalk snow removal begins at daylight. Everyone can't be first.
- ☐ Do not put yourself at risk unless it is an absolute emergency.

- ☐ Winter parking procedures were instituted to enable more timely and efficient removal of snow and ice. Management expects community residents to follow these parking procedures and plans its snow removal strategy accordingly.
- ☐ All vehicles should be parked at the sidewalk (curbside) without the vehicle extending over the curb. Don't back into your parking spot as it is better to

have your front-wheel-drive vehicle's front wheels where snow and ice can't be plowed against them.

☐ After the snowplow makes its first pass through the community and cleans the street and visitor parking area, residents should move their vehicles to the visitor parking area. Then the snowplow can clear the curbside parking spaces on its second pass through the community. No, you don't have to worry about moving your vehicle between 9:00 p.m. and 7:00 a.m.

☐ If you do not move your vehicle so that the plow(s) can clear the curbside parking spots in the most efficient manner, your non-compliance will be noted by management and you may be fined. Such fines help defray the cost of third and fourth plowings that become necessary because of non-compliance.

Storm Procedures for Older Residents

Some people have special physical circumstances that make storm parking compliance more difficult and dangerous. But the fact remains that it is still the resident's responsibility to get the necessary assistance. If a resident has medical assistance coming to the home on a regular basis, they need to make sure all workers are aware of the winter storm procedures as well.

Any resident needing assistance with complying with an association policy, procedure, or daily living routine should approach neighbors, family, friends, or paid help before calling the association's office for assistance. Sometimes the maintenance staff or management volunteers may be able to help those in need but they shouldn't be expected to help.

Icicles must be removed to save gutters

Chapter 18

VEHICULAR CHALLENGES

As a condominium manager, I was frequently called upon by residents to do something about the speeders and anti-one-way drivers in the community. Let's think about those requests. What could I do to curb this reckless driving? I am not a policeman with a siren and lights on my vehicle. However, I am not beyond challenges that would cause most people to look away, especially when I feel that I'm on the reasonably correct side of an issue.

Speeding

In many communities, some of the streets may be patrolled by the township or city police. Whatever happens to speeders and stop sign violators is out of the community's control. However, throughout any given year, the maintenance staff and I witnessed speeding and carelessness in parking lots and community-owned roads as we performed our work. One really can't label such carelessness as a "violation" since there are few speeding signs and no legitimate police enforcement through the parking lots. Like many other aspects of community association living, common sense and respect for neighbors should be the rule of the day. Fifteen to twenty miles per hour is a sensible operating speed throughout most communities. You never know when someone might back out of a parking spot or be going against the one-way traffic.

Personally speaking, I know very well what fifteen miles per hour looks and feels like. Over the past twenty-five years I have ridden my bicycle more than 100,000 miles, at an average speed of fifteen to twenty miles per hour. I know when someone is going faster than a bicycle through a parking lot. But I can't do anything about it except visit the inconsiderate or unthinking perpetrators and read them the riot act on common sense. Residents of a community must not be afraid to police their neighbors' careless driving by identifying the guilty (names and license number) and reporting such information to management. The neighborhood watch signs in the community should apply to all forms of behavior that threaten the safety of residents.

Residents shouldn't need speed signs and stop signs to tell them what acceptable driving behavior should be. But unless all of the residents police themselves, they risk the arrival of a police force composed of a lot of ugly signage and everyone's favorite—speed bumps.

Reckless Driving

Since no amount of traffic signage seems to work, and most community residents don't want fifty to sixty speed bumps in their community, here's what I do to deter reckless driving in parking areas and drives. When I spot a reckless driver, I usually stop them (that's the hard part) and give them a deterrence experience. Some experiences are better received than others, but I am always prepared to deal with the confrontational consequences.

In one community I managed, there is a one-way sign right in front of the management office area off the main drive. The sign has a big arrow that points to the right. It also has a fluorescent orange traffic cone in front of it. So most drivers would get the message that it's probably a good idea to go right. Even if they're just stopping to put trash in the maintenance yard dumpster, they should go around to the right. The maintenance trucks coming out of the yard are not expecting vehicles to approach from the wrong way! As far as I know, no one has ever been fined by management for reckless driving in the community. The rules and regulations do not offer such authority. Deterrence is the only possible remedy, and it's only as effective as the community's rules and the manager's chutzpah. Perhaps those rules and regulations can be tightened up a bit (a strict traffic fine enforcement policy).

Parking

I'm not sure which condo communities have fewer parking problems: those with designated parking spots or those without. Once I was instructed by a board of directors to paint unit numbers in parking spots to solve an ongoing parking issue. That was a couple of months before the board elections. Shortly after the elections, the new board instructed me to black out the numbers. It's difficult to get two people to agree on the best parking strategy in a condominium community, let alone two different executive boards. Here are some of my observations:

- ☐ Larger communities have more success (less trouble) with first come-first served random parking—of course with the exception of handicapped parking.
- ☐ Small communities do better with numbered or designated spots.
- ☐ All communities should have designated and well-marked visitor parking areas.
- ☐ All communities should have an association member vehicle registry which includes vehicle type, license plate number, and contact information.
- ☐ All communities should have a winter storm parking policy that enables efficient snow removal.
- ☐ Handicapped spaces should comply with ADA standards to avoid liability exposure.
- ☐ If necessary, educate community residents that the parking goal is to get the vehicle equidistant between the lines on both sides of the vehicle or the front and back of the vehicle.
- ☐ Residents should not complain about vehicle dings and dents if their vehicle was parked diagonally in a rectangular space.
- ☐ Make sure to look both ways when exiting a parking space, even if there is a one-way street through the parking lot. Don't assume that others see, remember, or follow one-way directions.

It's tough to enforce parking policy in condo communities. Verification of violations with photo evidence is a time consuming, tedious, and potentially confrontational exercise (being seen taking pictures).

Be careful if your last line of defense is to have a vehicle towed from your community. I consulted with a small association whose board president had a vehicle improperly towed from the community. The vehicle, a Mercedes, belonged to a physician who sued the association for $85,000 and won. Association members were special-assessed to cover the bill. Such parking violation battles should be picked wisely, especially if the accused has a big ego and deep pockets!

Handicap Parking

For seventeen years of my life, my main hobby was licensed bicycle road racing. In 1994, at the age of forty-five, I won a handicap race in Red Bank, New Jersey. It was one of my best performances ever. But what was my handicap? My age. You see, it was a race that included both "dinosaurs" (45 and older) and "studs" (18 to 24) competing against each other. The dinosaurs were given a two-minute head start "handicap" in a twenty-five-mile street circuit race. To my surprise, I won the race in a photo finish. My so-called handicap was actually an advantage—at least in my mind.

A physical handicap classification is not always what it appears to be. The reasons for handicap status are many and varied—ambulatory, respiratory, circulatory, temporary injury, etc. "Handicap" can also be a relative term. Some people are more handicapped than others.

My own dad and mom who lived their last twelve and nineteen years respectively at Glencreek were both wheel-chair bound. When I would look for a handicap parking space for my dad, he would scoff at me and state that he was not handicapped. He said that pushing him was good exercise. My mom was prone to take a little more advantage of her non-ambulatory condition.

I once did a study of a large, high-rise condo building. When I drove onto the building site, the first thing I noticed was hundreds of blue and white handicapped parking signs. The entire perimeter circle around the building was handicap spaces. Beyond that, all of the most convenient parking was also handicap designated. I thought it must have been an assisted-living community, but it wasn't. These spaces were probably authorized—whether legitimately or not was another issue.

I predict that the day will come (when baby boomers enter their feeble years) that there won't be enough handicap parking. Spaces will have to be color coded based on handicap severity. Until then, using a handicap space requires some conscience and consideration for the less fortunate. If you can walk your dog around the block, you can probably park a few more feet from your destination.

Certain areas, like the clubhouse and the pool, are limited in space for handicap parking. So when you pull up to that most convenient handicap space, ask yourself, "Could someone arrive after me who is more severely handicapped?" If the answer is "yes," then take the advantage of your less severe handicap and go the extra distance. In a perfectly unselfish world, the most convenient handicap parking space would always be empty.

Chapter 19

AMERICAN FLAGS
RESPECT AND HONOR

Appreciate and Accommodate

My experience has shown me that communities should do their best to be veteran and military friendly. That's why I recommend that condo boards should pick their battles very carefully when it comes to the display of the United States flag in their communities. One thing is for sure: you don't want to be the ones preventing the display of an American flag. For example, you absolutely don't want to pick such a battle with a veteran of the Armed Forces who is a member of your association and also has deep pockets. This is a potential lose-lose situation: lose the public relations battle and lose association funds to defend your unpopular stance.

Having said this, an association can control the size of a displayed flag and its manner of placement in the community. Perhaps a three foot by five foot flag is the maximum size that a community will allow. The placement of the flag can either be provided by the association or approved by the association. Some communities tend toward a standard placement at all units. Other communities may allow more random placement with approval from the board. Whatever the case, flag controls should work within the layout of your community architecture and landscaping.

I always try to get some type of flag installation at the community entrance or another acceptable location within the communities I manage, because I feel it's important to honor the service and sacrifice of those who have put their lives on the line for us. I spearheaded and helped build the veterans memorial patio to honor deceased veterans who had lived in one of the communities I managed. It was a volunteer project funded by community charitable donations. We found a space for the memorial in place of a trash dumpster pad that was moved to an enclosed maintenance yard. One feature of the patio was a thirty foot flagpole. Since the completion of this patriotic project fifteen years ago, there has never been a flag issue or flag policy challenge in that community.

Veterans Memorial Project 2005

The Veterans Memorial Project began with a generous donation from a longtime resident, in honor of her husband who passed away in 2004. The contribution covered the cost and installation of a thirty-foot flagpole and name plaque. The rest of the memorial project area surrounding the pole involved the construction of a stone-paved patio, benches, lighting, and some landscaping. The association received $6,500 from residents and contractors to finance the project.

Good progress was made on the Glencreek Veterans Memorial Project during the month of August. The stone patio and composite access ramp was completed. Lights were installed with a dawn-to-dusk timer which ensured that the flag would be lit throughout the night hours. Glencreek's landscaper donated and planted shrubbery around the patio. Railings and benches were donated by residents and board members who wished to become part of the meaningful and patriotically fulfilling project.

The memorial was completed by November 11, 2005. At the dedication ceremony on Veterans Day, the local state representative spoke. Despite the fact that the coldest part of the day was during the forty-five minute ceremony, approximately 100 guests braved the elements and were treated afterward to a nice luncheon in the warmth of the Glencreek Clubhouse. A great setting, good oratory, patriotic music, and military etiquette contributed to the impressive dedication. Management received many calls and notes of thanks for this patriotic addition to our property.

From the Manager's Desk:

A Red, White, and Blue Observation

As I make my rounds in the community, I can't help but notice the abundance of American flags on display. Several units have several flags. There is no doubt about our level of patriotism. The main catalyst for the current swell of patriotism is the U.S. anti-terrorism action in Afghanistan and Iraq. Everyone wants to support the troops (perhaps family or relatives) who are in harm's way.

As the Glencreek property manager, I look around and wonder, "Can you have too much patriotism?" Probably not, I think. Then I ask, "Can you have too many flags displayed?" The answer is, "Yes." The Glencreek Rules and Regulations Guidebook is clear on this issue. Our rules stipulate that "decorative flags are prohibited with the following exceptions. An American flag is permitted, but may not be attached to fences. Maintenance must install them at the appropriate location."

Any owner who already has an approved flag installation and wants to show more patriotic spirit is welcome to get involved with the Glencreek Veterans Memorial Patio project. Enhancements for, contributions to, and maintenance of the memorial area are some of the ways people can show their patriotic spirit. The flagpole on the patio is everyone's to share.

Chapter 20

PET PEEVES

Pets can cause problems for condo associations, but dealing with family pet issues in a condo community is controllable. Problems with number, noise, size, breed, control, and excretions are generally addressed in the association resident's manual in the section on pet policies. In addition, the municipality where the condo community is located may have its own pet policy (a.k.a. leash law).

When you apply pet compliance justice equally, legal entanglements will be minimal.

A municipal leash law takes precedence over condo owner policy, but the condo policy may be more restrictive if necessary. Although it can be stricter, it can't be more lenient. Just remember that pet policy compliance issues have to be corrected in a fair and consistent manner after proper notification. When you apply pet compliance justice equally, legal entanglements will be minimal.

Dogs

If a UFO hovered over any suburban community in the United States, what would the aliens see? Morning, noon, and night, they'd see a four-legged species leading a two-legged species by a leash attached to its hand. The four-legged species would excrete bodily waste whenever and wherever it wanted, and the two-legged species would examine it, pick it up, and carry it all the way back to the house. Who would the aliens think was the dominant earth species?

I was raised in a place and time when most dogs were free range and they seemed to love it. Many were hunting dogs. Personally, if I had been forced to pick up my hunting dogs' poop, I would have given up hunting. The dogs had a comfortable outside dog house and were fed scraps from the dinner table. If we liked our family meals, the dogs lost weight. If necessary, we'd get a can of dog food from our family grocery store shelves to supplement the canine nourishment. When the temperature was below ten degrees, we'd let the dogs stay in the garage.

Be careful when dealing with dogs and dog owners. Their issues will attract legal battles faster than fleas.

The only downside to having free-range dogs was that the dogs occasionally were hit by cars because we lived along a main county route. Our cats suffered similar fates. None of them had nine lives. On more than one occasion my dad woke me up early in the morning with the instructions, "Get up, go out, and shovel the cat off the highway before your sisters wake up." Needless to say, we went through more dogs and cats than modern-day families.

I won't deny that I have a difficult time adjusting to the four-legged pet empathy of modern society. It takes a conscientious effort for me to be compassionate to dog owners whose dogs are considered children—family members. In the ninth grade, I had a friend whose grandmother lived with the family. She had a Pomeranian that wore a diaper and sat in a high chair at family meals—and that was in 1963. I thought she was crazy.

Nonetheless, if you're going to be a successful condo manager you have to get along with dogs and dog owners, because there are many of them. Condo dog policies, with their rules and regulations, vary widely. Community demographics, architecture, plot plans, and geographical location are some of the major factors affecting the management of dogs and dog owners.

All I can say is, be careful when dealing with dogs and dog owners. Their issues will attract legal battles faster than fleas. If the dog owners are willing to spend thousands of dollars on doggie healthcare (shots, spaying, surgery, etc.), what makes you think that the cost of a lawsuit will deter them from defending a precious pooch in canine court?

Condo boards should adapt the association pet policy to the community's demographic and surroundings. For example, if your community has a mostly elderly demographic but there are also some younger residents, some of the stereotypical breeds that have, rightly or wrongly, gained a troublemaking reputation should be disallowed.

I managed a community with an older demographic, but one younger resident had a pit bull. While I was visiting the community to do a weekly inspection at this resident's building, the pit bull, which I thought was leashed, came after me. Generally, I'm not afraid of dogs. I stopped in my tracks. The dog ran right to my feet and stopped, while growling fiercely. The dog's owner, a large young man, came running after the dog yelling, "He won't hurt you! He won't hurt you! Don't move!" I answered him by asking him, "Yeah, but who's gonna pay for cleaning the mess in my pants?" I happened to be a tough old man who didn't scare easily. Suppose that dog ran up to a little old lady and she fell down or had a heart attack?

There are good reasons for strict dog policies in a condo community. People don't want to be special-assessed for a costly lawsuit because of the negligence of one dog owner. A dog's bark may be worse than its bite, but sometimes the bark is simply enough to cause severe injury.

Cats

The term "house cat" would seem to define where a pet cat should stay, but many owners allow their pet cats outside. In addition to the problems domesticated cats can create among residents, many condo communities experience feral cat invasions. There can be a number of reasons for this phenomenon, most of them man-made. The community may be a drop-off area for unwanted cats if it is in close proximity to a park or a secluded area. Residents may take pity on scrawny stray cats and feed them out of compassion, while stopping short of adopting them and keeping them indoors. Community residents may even lose their pet cats and start feeding the feral cats as replacement pets.

Unchecked, feral cat colonies can multiply about as fast as rabbits. They don't have many natural predators. Current trap neuter release (TNR) programs can help slow down the proliferation of cats, but that still does not solve the problems caused by the cats. Mainly, you can neuter a cat to prevent kittens, but they still are able to kill birds and excrete their feces in private yard areas. Unless the cats get colostomies and can figure out how to empty their bags in a designated area, you're not going to solve that cat problem.

During a six-month period in my association management history, I trapped ninety-seven feral cats in one community. One resident would put out seven bowls of food each night without coming out of her house. She would open her bedroom window and put the bowls on the ground behind a large shrub. In the morning she would retrieve the bowls from the window. She didn't think I noticed. When confronted about her cat feeding process, she denied doing it. I asked her, "Why is your recycle bin filled with empty Friskies cans?" (There were about ninety.) She confessed, because she didn't have any of her own pet cats. In this particular situation, there were regulations regarding feral cats and fines for noncompliance. The local township also had a strict feral cat policy. To this day, there are still feral cat problems in this community.

For a while I had gotten in the habit of taking photos of all the feral cats that I trapped. Once I trapped a feral kitten, but did not have my camera with me. While I went to my office to retrieve my camera, one of the unit owners stole my trap with the cat inside. I was curious about the kit-napping, but did not pursue the issue. About a week later, I received a phone call from an upset unit owner who confessed to taking my trap. She saw the cat in the trap and took it to her second floor unit. She planned to domesticate it, but that didn't go too well. When the cat was let out of the trap, it ran into the bathroom and went down in the hollow core concrete flooring through a hole next to the bathroom sink pipe.

This unit owner called me to apologize, but also to help her solve the problem: get the cat out of the floor before it died. When it was all said and done, this woman's effort to domesticate a feral cat cost her about $400. I thought that she had probably learned her lesson, until she came to me about two years later with her solution to the ongoing feral cat problem in the community. She suggested that the community participate in the TNR program and at the same time build a feral cat gazebo where concerned residents could deposit food and water for the cats to eat and socialize with each other (the cats, that is). According to her, the cats would build a strong feral cat family that would protect their gazebo and community from new non-neutered arrivals.

Unchecked, feral cat colonies can multiply about as fast as rabbits. They don't have many natural predators.

I eventually told this concerned cat lover that if she would get her friends to finance and complete her small cat condo in a remote area of the community, it would be okay. I haven't heard anything about this project in over five years. I guess it didn't have another life.

Meanwhile, the executive board set up a "kitty" for donations for the TNR program. At the same time the TNR was taking place, owners and residents were asked not to feed feral cats. Although the TNR program helped control the feral cat population in the community, it still didn't solve all of the problems associated with cats that are allowed outside: excrement and odor in the planting beds adjacent to the residences.

Chapter 21

CRITTER CONCERNS

Wild animals such as squirrels, waterfowl, rodents, insects, snakes, birds of prey, raccoons, opossums, foxes, and deer are all critters that a condo community may have to deal with, depending on its geographic location. The nature of a community and its amenities (ponds, nature trails, etc.) will determine the challenges. If your condo is in Maine, you could have a moose problem; in Florida, alligators; in Alaska, bears...

If the board members are tree-hugging, animal rights activists with a more urban background, wildlife problems will be magnified and expensive to remedy.

If the association manager has a strong country background and understands nature's nuances, the critter problems in the community will be minimized and solved less expensively. However, if the manager or board members are tree-hugging, animal rights activists with a more urban background, the wildlife problems will be magnified and expensive to remedy. In either instance, the board must have a solid understanding of the community and its opinion on critter issues.

I have gone ten rounds with overzealous naturalists many times over the years. I've never been afraid to engage in a conversation with ORCA (Organization for Responsible Care of Animals) or the SPCA (Society for the Prevention of Cruelty to Animals). They never had it easy with me because my country-boy, nature-loving, been-there-done-that background was too intimidating.

The kind of wildlife wisdom that I've acquired is rare in today's society. Managers like me are a dying breed. When we are totally extinct, the critter problems and their associated costs will greatly increase. People eventually learn the important lessons of life through their wallet or through physical pain. Dealing with critter issues is no different.

Squirrels

Squirrels are a typical problem that many condo associations in the Northeast United States have to deal with in some manner. I experienced it first-hand in a large community that had a lot of mature oaks and walnut trees, with acorns and walnuts galore. There were hundreds (if not thousands) of squirrels. They caused a variety of problems from home invasion to eating vehicle wires and hoses.

As the association manager, I never did much about such issues, considering the number of complaints I received. Yes, I made sure that the building damage was repaired after ascertaining that the squirrels were out of the building. I welcomed the red-tailed hawks whose regular diet included squirrels. I even loaned animal traps to individual owners upon request. I did nothing about squirrels attacking vehicle parts except advising residents that the squirrels seemed to prefer older model Chrysler products and that perhaps a new car was due.

Squirrels are a migratory species. No, they don't go to Miami in the winter; they migrate to the areas with the most food. If a condo community has an abundance of nuts (acorns, not people), there are going to be a lot of squirrels. Get rid of the nut-bearing trees and the squirrel population decreases. But what are the tree huggers going to say? They'll be torn apart if they're also squirrel lovers. Welcome to the nutty world of condo management and living.

From the Managers Desk: A Tale of Six Tails

I thought I had seen it all until one day when our mail carrier came into my office to tell me he had seen something disturbing in front of Unit 5. He was distraught and asked if I would help him out. Together we went to Unit 5 and there, under a large, old oak tree, were six half-grown squirrels spinning like a whirling dervish. Upon closer inspection, I saw that the squirrels' tails were all tangled up in one big knot, woven so tightly with fur and nest debris that the individual tails weren't distinguishable. The squirrels were quite literally end to end to end to end to end to end.

I asked the mail carrier to keep an eye on the artificially conjoined sextuplets while I retrieved a pair of hedge trimmers from our maintenance shop. When I returned to the scene, a small crowd had gathered to witness a first for our community: tail separation surgery. With a tree limb, the mail carrier held down the flailing mass of gray fur, while I began poking, picking, and snipping. After about ten minutes of dealing with the squirming and squealing mass, I'd accomplished little.

"Just throw them in the pond," one bystander shouted. "We've got too many squirrels around here anyway." I agreed, but kept snipping. Still nothing.

From what I knew, a squirrel could survive without its tail, or with only a part of it. So I opened up the trimmers, positioned them carefully around the most distinct section of fur, and snapped them shut. To my amazement, one squirrel immediately ran free. His tail was drastically shortened, but he would survive. And freeing him had loosened the knot a bit.

Encouraged, I started in again. Five minutes later, a second squirrel scampered free, tail completely intact.

Then came the third, fourth, fifth, and sixth squirrels—
all relatively unharmed and eager to get away from their
two-legged neighbors.

In all my time in and around this community, I've
never experienced such a bizarre display of animal
behavior. But then again, how many managers can add
"squirrel untangler" to their resume?

Koi Polloi

Common carp were first bred for color in Japan in the 1820s.
The rest of the world was not aware of the development of koi
until 1914 when they were exhibited at the annual exposition
in Tokyo. In Japanese, koi is a homophone for another word
that means "affection" or "love." Koi are therefore symbols
of love and friendship in Japan.

Koi are an ornamental variety of domesticated carp that
are kept for decorative purposes in ponds or water gardens.
They exhibit a variety of striking colors, which puts them at
a severe disadvantage against predators. Herons, kingfishers,
raccoons, cats, and foxes are all capable of successfully
fishing in a pond that contains koi.

There is plenty of information online about the proper
care of koi and koi ponds. Koi are a very hardy breed and can
survive in almost any climate as long as their basic needs are
met, the primary need being enough oxygen in their water.
Koi are omnivorous fish, eating a variety of foods including
bread, peas, lettuce, watermelons, and worms on a hook.
They can be trained to take food from one's hand. With additional effort, they can be taught to roll over and speak. In the
winter, their digestive systems slow nearly to a halt, and they
eat very little except a few nibbles of algae from the bottom
and an occasional pizza from a delivery man driving into
the pond. Their appetites do not come back until the water
becomes warm in the spring.

At one of my communities, there is no planned care of
the koi and their environment (a one-quarter acre pond).

However, the water is highly oxygenated for eight months of the year as a result of two decorative aerating fountains. Their food nourishment comes naturally or from visiting spectators. They survive every winter season, many under a thin coat of ice. The original koi in this pond are over thirty years old, very large, and obviously very healthy.

Venison, Anyone?

A couple of days after the official close of the Pennsylvania whitetail deer hunting season, I was doing paperwork in the Glencreek office when the mailman told me that he saw a "nice buck" in the cornfield along Glencreek Drive. I said, "Whatta ya mean by nice . . . friendly?" The mailman said, "No, big antlers!" So I hustled outside to get a look at the beautiful creature, it being that I had not shot a buck that year and am an avid outdoorsman.

The deer wasn't in the cornfield anymore, so I sneaked across the field with the wind in my face into the little patch of woods visible from Glencreek Drive. Sure enough, in a thicket of brush about twenty yards away was a magnificent ten-point buck. The antlers were practically white, which made them visible with every movement of the deer's head. I got to within about twenty feet of the buck before he noticed me. He then calmly exited the woods and crossed the road near the local Catholic Church into the northeast area of Landis Woods. Hopefully, when that big buck meets his demise, it will be in the sights of an outdoor sportsman and not at the front end of a vehicular surprise!

Have Gun, Will Travel

Unbeknownst to most everyone until now, I have been licensed to "pack heat" for almost twenty years. I do not carry my pistol 24/7, but only when I think it might come in handy do I holster up. Originally, I bought a pistol for hunting, fishing, and target shooting. Fishing, you ask? Yes, in the spring I fish for wild trout in the Catskill Mountains. I never know when I might run into a sow bear with cubs. That bear will not run if I cast my lure at it. Eventually, I got licensed to carry a pistol for self-protection. I never envisioned a situation where I would need firearm protection until the board elections of 2014. [See Chapter 24.] I just wanted to be able to help to protect others if necessary.

About ten years ago, I was traveling a local interstate highway when I witnessed a vehicle hit a doe that was being chased by a buck during the mating season. Hunters like me are alert to such deer behavior in late autumn in the Northeast. The driver blasted the deer, disabling his vehicle and causing a large traffic jam. I drove up the shoulder of the road with my jeep, jumped out, and immediately recognized that the deer was injured beyond recovery. The driver was flustered and incapable of self-help. As he sat in his small vehicle with his cell phone in hand, I instructed him to turn on his ignition so he could steer as I pushed his car to the highway shoulder. As he sat there trying to call someone, I returned to my jeep, retrieved my pistol, walked up to the wounded deer, and put two bullets in its head. I grabbed a leg and dragged the deer off the road. Then I hustled around and picked up some scattered car parts and signaled the backed-up traffic to move out—all of this with an astonished audience and not one other volunteer helper. Excited and out of breath, I rested against my jeep as the passing motorists gave me their "thumbs up" to thank me. I don't know if an ambulance or policeman showed up that day. They really didn't have to, since I cleaned up the mess.

When I knew I was right, I was not afraid to take control of a situation. I was willing to own the problem, for better or worse.

Now you begin to see why I was the type of condo association manager who was not afraid to take the bull (or the deer) by the horns without hesitation. When I knew I was right, I was not afraid to take control of a situation. I was willing to own the problem, for better or worse. Right is right and wrong is wrong, and if you waste too much time thinking, there can be unnecessary suffering, personal or property damage, or even death.

Anyway, while in the possession of my pistol one day, I was approached by a member of the landscaping crew. He said there was a wounded feral cat on the property. It had been hit by a car. Upon arrival at the scene, I found a big black feral cat with a broken back and some visible insides that were outside its body. Two young men, also of the land-scape crew, stood about twenty feet away staring in horror at the hissing cat. Perhaps they never experienced such animal trauma before. It was not pretty.

Without telegraphing my intentions, I walked up to the cat, drew my hidden pistol, and promptly ended its ninth life. Later on that day, I was at my office working on the annual financial statements when the owner of the landscaping company visited me. Light-heartedly, he expressed to me that I had made a lasting impression on his two workers who witnessed my kind act of feline euthanasia. These two young men said to their boss, "Man, you do not want to fuck with that guy!" This incident showed me that a little intimidation can go a long way in the condo association management industry.

Waterfowl

Have you ever had to clean goose poop off your sidewalk or driveway or vehicle? If so, you would likely rather not do it on a regular basis. If your community has a pond or a lake, there's a good chance you'll have a problem with geese from time to time. At a minimum, you'll have goose excrement in all the grassy areas adjacent to the water, and it will eventually be on the soles of your shoes.

So how do you get rid of the geese? Well, if they're migratory geese, your problem will be temporary, although still messy. If your goose population doesn't fly south for the winter or north for the summer, your problem may approach permanency.

As a manager of communities with ponds, my solution was a pistol. Whenever I saw more than five geese in the pond, I shot my pistol into the ground. The geese flew away, as they react instinctively to predator gunfire. Their instincts are sharp and the pistol worked.

One time I was watering some flowers near the management office and some geese wandered close by and made a fecal deposit on the sidewalk. I sprayed the hose on them, and they ran away. Unfortunately, a female resident saw me spraying water on the geese and threatened to call ORCA. Go figure. I guess she thought geese don't like unexpected showers.

There are many ways to get rid of geese on your property. Barking will make them scatter. If I'm out of bullets, I bark. It's worse than my bite. Statues of dogs, people, and foxes by the pond may work for a while. Eventually these gimmicks destroy the aesthetic beauty of the setting. If it gets to the point that you're considering hiring a goose consultant, it's probably cheaper to drain your pond and fill it in.

Ducks are a different matter. I found them to be less troublesome than geese, but my solutions were the same, unless the ducks were decoys. One community pond had fountains operating for eight months of the year. When the fountains were removed for the winter, the underwater electric wires had to be secured in a way that made them identifiable and accessible come spring when the fountains were re-installed. So for years we used empty milk jugs as flotation markers to which the electrical wires were attached. But management got tired of residents and passersby complaining about the trash (the empty milk jugs) floating in the pond. So I went to the sporting goods store and bought half a dozen duck decoys. The floating duck decoys took the place of the milk jugs—a much more aesthetically appealing scene.

Well, when the cold weather came, the decoys were frozen in the pond with little snowcaps on their heads. The next thing you know, the management office starts getting phone calls that there are ducks frozen in the pond and if they can't fly, they will die. Thirty to forty calls were received in the first few years—some threatening to turn us in for cruelty to animals. And that wasn't the end of it. Passersby would try to feed the ducks with bread crumbs or throw stones in the water to get them to move. Once a Chinese tour bus stopped and took pictures of the ducks. On another occasion, a couple went out on the one-inch thick ice with a plastic shovel to "rescue" the ducks. I understand that such bizarre behavior still takes place, albeit less frequently. Humans should realize that if it doesn't walk like a duck, quack like a duck, or fly like a duck, then it's probably not a real duck!

Hawk and Squirrel

Trees, Squirrels, Cars, and People
By Leo Rosenberger

Trees that are beautiful can also cause a mess
On cars, lots, walks, and lawns, creating management stress.
Perhaps there are too many trees, especially the oaken kind.
If some of them were taken down, how many people would mind?

People love to look at trees. They also enjoy the shade.
Squirrels love trees even more; that's where their homes are made.
Squirrels would be more tolerable if their numbers were fewer.
But appreciation of Mother Nature depends upon the viewer.

Too many squirrels in Glencreek, and not enough food to eat
Their hunger is disabling cars, and they're not easy to defeat.
Cars are a people necessity, but expensive to repair
The squirrels are simply hungry. Of damage, they're unaware.

More trees, less squirrels, and cars that work are wanted at our estates.
But the board has to make the decisions that affect our fates
So squirrels love Glencreek, but people do, too.
If you were the manager, what would you do?

Chapter 22

WHERE HAVE ALL THE OWNERS GONE?

Leasing Concerns

Generally speaking, there is a direct correlation between the number of problems in condo communities and the number of leased condos in a community. Ask any condo board or manager which units are the most troublesome in their community. Almost exclusively, the answer will be the rented condo units.

Enforcing tenant compliance to community policies and procedures is extremely difficult. The number of tenants who actually read the condo resident's manual is minuscule. Ultimately, the behavior of tenants is the responsibility of their landlords. But in many cases, condo landlords are absentee owners who just don't have a bond with the community. Their major concern is the collection of their rents. As long as a condo tenant doesn't trash the inside of the unit and pays the rent, you'll hardly ever hear from the absentee owner, especially if he lives out of state.

Over the years, I've never received much interest from condo investors regarding any association community issues. I don't think they were even too concerned with the expense side of the association financial statements although it was crucial to their investment success.

But what happens when the tenant doesn't follow the condo association's policies and procedures? The manager must deal with both parties. This is because the tenant (who has no financial stake in the community) usually blows the manager off. Consequently, the manager has to deal with tenant issues through the absentee owner, who may be difficult to contact. Since the association contract is with the owner and not his or her tenants, the owner should be notified to bring his tenant(s) into compliance with association policy. It can take a long time to solve a tenant problem through the intermediary of the absentee owner.

Boards must be diligent in keeping rental unit files up-to-date. A current lease should always be on file. You would be surprised how many things can change inside a rental unit when you're not paying attention.

Community Rental Limitations

The largest community I ever managed enacted a rental limitation amendment in 2008. It did so because the number of rental units was approaching twenty-five percent of the total units in the community. Mortgagors, banks, and the FHA do not like to see a high percentage of rental units in condo association communities. In fact, the FHA will not approve loans for prospective buyers when rental percentages are too high.

The aforementioned community's amendment called for a ten percent limit on leased units. One out-of-state investor who owned ten leased units was not happy when the amendment was passed. Why? Because when he decides to sell his units, he'd like to sell them as a block to another investor. But he can't because if he sells, it has to be a sale to buyers who are going to live in the community. That will make the sale of his units more tedious, time consuming, and probably, less profitable. After a period of six years, the number of rentals decreased from ninety to sixty.

Boards must realize that investors and their realtor representatives do not like rental limitation clauses in condo documents. Realtors are interested in sales, and investors are interested in profits, condo association policy be damned. Realtors will offer the logic that limiting sales that are available to investors will depress market values. I don't know how many times I've been told by a realtor that he could have sold a property several times if he had been allowed to sell it to an investor. When it comes to their real estate commissions, the unscrupulous have tunnel vision.

As a seasoned board member and manager, my contention is that a high percentage of investor units (rentals) actually depresses community market values. The quality of tenancy in condo associations is usually poor and leads to a diverse set of problems. In a condo community you want a fairly homogeneous group of owners who can afford the lifestyle and are proud of their community. What you don't want is *Condo boards should make sure that their association leasing policy is tight, with no legal loopholes.* a bunch of landlords with tenants who just get by. There are some exceptional investor landlords, but my experience has shown that they are in a minority.

Condo boards should make sure that their association leasing policy is tight, with no legal loopholes. The association resident's manual should cover all situations that the declaration and bylaws do not. The key word here is "all." Every time I thought I'd seen it "all," another quirky incident popped up. Managers must closely monitor condo tenant behavior so that situations don't get out of control.

What types of situations could be that complicated or sensitive to cause a board a lot of trouble? How about tenants smoking marijuana on a regular basis? Is this a landlord issue, an association board issue, or a police issue? Or is it a health code issue? Doing some weed in a detached home out in the country is one thing, but in a multi-unit condo building where the smoke and odor infiltrates other units is a multi-faceted problem. Who calls the police into the situation: the landlord, the upset neighbors, or the association manager? Do you begin to see the picture? Any problem is a greater problem in a condo community.

Atypical Living Arrangements

Atypical living arrangements in a condo community can be even more problematic than rentals. Why? Because if a resident isn't an owner or a tenant under lease, then what kind of jurisdiction does the association have over such a living arrangement when the maverick resident causes problems? The following are two different real-life examples of the difficulties brought on by unthinking and/or sly owners.

In order to bypass an association rental limitation policy, a married couple purchased a condo and included their daughter on the deed of ownership. The daughter ended up living by herself in the unit. Putting their daughter on the deed was technically legal, but in reality just a token ownership interest for her. If her name was not on the deed, the association would consider her a tenant, whether she paid rent or not to her parents. Money does not have to change hands for a legal tenant relationship to exist.

To further complicate this situation, when the daughter went on an extended career-related tour, her girlfriend moved in under the guise of being her cat sitter. When confronted by me, the manager, with the reality of the situation, the parent-owners had a conniption fit. They got a lawyer relative on the other side of the country to come after me. Resolving this situation took a $150 conversation and letter from the association's attorney to convince the parent-owners of the absurdity of the contrived living arrangements. Case closed.

The second example of an atypical living arrangement occurred when a female unit owner invited her male friend to be a permanent resident in her unit. Had he just lived in her unit quietly, a problem would never have developed. After he had resided in the community for a while, we forgot about his nonmember status in the condo association. He wasn't an owner or a tenant. He was just a resident with his lady friend's mailing address. The association had no legal jurisdiction over, or contract with, him. He was sort of in condo limbo.

Sometime later this individual came under the spell of a disgruntled minority element in the community and began to shoot off his mouth (especially when inebriated). The straw that broke the camel's back was his appearance at an association-members-only open board meeting where he became disruptive.

Though allowed to remain at the meeting (no constable was present), he was denied entry at the next open meeting by a hired constable. Then this misinformed troublemaker retained his friend's overzealous attorney, who threatened to sue the association for violating his client's first amendment right to free speech. Once again, the association was forced to spend a couple hundred dollars for its legal counsel to send a letter explaining the errors of the attacking attorney's accusation. Case closed.

Are you beginning to understand the time and money that is wasted by associations that have to deal with tenants and weird living arrangements in a condo community? There was a third ownership living arrangement that I experienced as a board member which led to a crime. Furthermore, it involved a dysfunctional board member. The details of that incident were so numerous and bizarre that they warrant their own chapter in this book. [See Chapter 24.]

Inevitably, as the association manager, I become part of the equation to solve lease and living arrangement problems—like it or not. I'm sort of the "X-factor."

Inevitably, as the association manager, I become part of the equation to solve lease and living arrangement problems. Like it or not, I'm sort of the X-factor. My solutions vary depending on the nature of the givens. For instance, if a unit owner decides to have an unrelated friend live in his unit instead of himself, such an arrangement is considered a lease. An exchange of money or services or a written agreement is not a prerequisite to a lease arrangement. Usually it does not matter what excuse is given for the arrangement (pet sitting, house sitting, job transfer, illness, etc.). When I encounter such blurry arrangements, I examine them closely and give consideration to extenuating circumstances. Remember, the reason for the association's lease limitation amendment isn't based on the amount of rent or any rent at all. It is based on not wanting too many absentee owners, who usually do not control their tenants.

Chapter 23

HOARDING STORIES

There is a country western song by Barbara Mandrell titled "I Was Country When Country Wasn't Cool." Well, hoarding will never be "cool," but I was the manager of a community that had two serious hoarders when hoarders weren't even reality TV stars. They were sad cases and worthy of our compassion. In each instance, the local health agencies had to be called in to evaluate the sites and make recommendations.

An Illness of Varying Degree

Boards and managers have to be very careful when dealing with hoarding issues. These situations cannot be ignored because there are neighbors who could be put in harm's way. In addition to the obvious health issues, there could be insect, rodent, or pest (feral cats) infestations, not to mention the fire hazard of piles of clutter. Additionally, there could be damage as a result of neglected repairs (plumbing leaks, lack of heat, or proliferation of mold).

Health agencies or local law enforcement will give boards the direction and authority they need to enter a unit and abate the problem. Most condominium documents give boards and managers the legal authority for such situations without the risk of incurring a legal action for entering the unit. In my association, the board did not even have to give notice of such entry. Think about it. Is a hoarder going to answer the phone or respond to a mailed notice? No. They'll just throw the notice in with the rest of the trash in the unit.

My two experiences with hoarders were quite different. One was solved internally by the manager (me) and the board, but did require a judicial ruling by the local district justice. The second experience required help from health agencies and was the worst living situation I've ever encountered. This was far beyond the reality TV hoarders that you may see today. It took months to clear up the mess and save the hoarder's life.

Patio Pathos

My first experience with a hoarder involved a middle-aged single woman who had accumulated a large pile of junk that completely filled up her outdoor fence-enclosed patio. It became a feral cat hotel. Neighbors complained. Something had to be done. I knew it would be difficult because of past incidents in which she had been seen screaming at neighbors and community contractors. She actually got physical with the landscapers and yelled at me for operating a chainsaw in the woods adjacent to her unit. I'm not sure if she was on and off meds, but her behavior could change direction on a dime.

As the association manager, I began to issue warning notices that her patio had to be cleaned out. The first couple of notices were ignored. When she wasn't home, I took pictures of the mess on the patio. Her gate was not locked, and the condominium documents gave me the authority to enter and abate. I was not even required to serve notice of entry, because this was a limited common element owned by the association.

After about four months of notices, I decided to take more severe action. I got each board member to visit the hoarding site and see it for themselves. I explained everything to them, and they authorized me to clean it. I sent one final notice by certified mail. I told the unit owner that if it wasn't cleaned up by a deadline date, the association would enter the patio and clean it up at her expense. The certified notice came back to us unaccepted.

After the deadline passed, I waited for a day when I knew the hoarder was not at home. When that day came, I took two of my maintenance men to the site to begin the cleanup at 9:00 a.m. She had violated association policy and padlocked her patio gate. I expected such a stunt, grabbed my bolt cutters, and hopped over the patio fence.

I cut the lock, opened the gate, and the three of us attacked the cluttered pile of worthless junk in the patio area. We took before, during, and after pictures every step of the way. We filled the entire front yard with the hoarder's "valuable" possessions. It reminded me of digging a hole and throwing the dirt in a pile. When the hole is dug, the pile of dirt next to it is four times larger than the hole. How did all that dirt fit in that little hole?

As the hoarder's neighbors passed by during our cleanup, they were shocked at the amount of junk, but seemingly not surprised by who had accumulated it. After the patio was totally cleaned, we power washed everything, removing a few years of mold, mildew, animal feces, and God only knows what else. When we were finished we loaded all the debris into a wagon and brought it to the maintenance yard. There we unloaded it into a pile and covered it with a big tarpaulin.

I returned to the patio and took a final set of pictures. The patio looked like a picture in *Better Homes and Gardens*. The entire clean up had taken about three hours, and we finished before the hoarder returned home.

I heard that when she returned home and noticed the patio, she went ballistic. "They ruined my patio!" Really? About a week later, she got the cleanup bill of about $600. And two months later, we were headed to the district justice across the street to file a lien for the collection of the debt.

The association's attorney tried to broker a deal before entering into the judge's courtroom, but the hoarder and her attorney refused, thinking that their case against the association was airtight. The hearing was over fast. The judge reviewed our governing documents relating to the patio entry, looked at the warning notices, and compared the before and after photos. He addressed the hoarder and her attorney and asked, "So why are you here today?" Shortly thereafter, while the hoarder was in the midst of a lengthy tirade allowed by her attorney, the judge slammed down his gavel. Case closed: judgment in favor of the association. Not long afterwards, a trash collector hired by the hoarder showed up unannounced and took the entire pile of junk to the dump station. All of her valuable possessions ended up in the dump.

Eight years later this hoarder, a peculiar person to say the least, was right back at it. This time she attempted to have me arrested two days before the annual association meeting and election. She failed and the arresting officer got a departmental reprimand.

Life and Limb

About ten years ago, I walked into a situation that was as terrible as anyone could imagine. And guess what? It was a rental unit. The off-site owner (about sixty miles away) likely hadn't inspected the unit in years. To make the situation even more unbelievable, the hoarder was not an ignorant poor soul by any means. I later discovered that this gentleman had an IQ that was off the charts. He was a retired "madman." No, not a crazed condo maniac, but a person like those featured in the TV series "Madmen," which is about New York City's Madison Avenue advertising executives back in the 1950s.

I got suspicious about this unit one day when I noticed a car in the parking lot that was not properly inspected or registered with the state. Looking through the window into the vehicle, I could see that it was a vehicular trash dump. The car was filled with fast-food wrappers. I went back to the office to review the community vehicle registry to determine who owned the car. That's how I established the unit number of the resident.

I decided to take my maintenance supervisor with me to inspect the unit, fearing we might find a dead body inside. This was an upstairs unit in a two-story condo building. Upon entering the unit, we were immediately struck by a putrid stench that hit us like a Mack truck. My supervisor got sick and went back outside. Being used to such odors (having hunted, gutted, and skinned dead game animals), I continued up the stairs expecting to find a dead occupant.

At the top of the stairs I got my first view of what it must look like inside a large garbage truck. The entire main living and dining area had everything strewn around: newspapers, books (at least 1,000), clothes, food, signs, posters, and antiques. The unit's occupant was asleep on the sofa.

At this point, I started breathing through my mouth because of the vile odor. While he slept, I peeked in the bedroom and noticed that part of the drywall ceiling had fallen on the bed. The bathroom and kitchen couldn't have been cleaned in months, if not years. Back in the living room, the hoarder awakened and I talked to him. I found out he had a foot injury that was infected. It was ugly; something had to be done, and fast. I'm sure the other residents in the building would not want to know what they were living next to or beneath.

I called the out-of-town landlord and the local health authority to make them aware of the situation. It took about six months to clean up the mess inside the unit. The hoarder moved out and was taken care of through the health system, eventually losing the infected foot and leg. I'm not sure if he is still alive. It was a very sad experience, the likes of which I hope I will never see again.

Chapter 24

BAD BOYS, BAD GIRLS, WHATCHA GONNA DO?

A Cautionary Tale

A board member owned and lived in her unit. At some point she moved out and went to live with her boyfriend in a neighboring city. She still owned her condo in our community, and despite the distance, she remained on the board. Without board approval, she rented her unit to her stepparents. A couple of years later, her boyfriend bought a unit in our community and they moved back, living in his condo and leasing hers. Not long thereafter, the long-term, live-in boyfriend decided to run for a board position, which would bring his term (if elected) concurrent with hers.

The board checked with its attorney and though the bylaws didn't specifically say he couldn't serve concurrently, the attorney advised the board that their long-term living arrangement was virtually the same as being married. In essence, they would be stacking the board if he ran and won the election. In a letter with the attorney's endorsement, the board advised him and the members of the community that his bid for a board position was ill advised and would be detrimental to the association's governance. Nonetheless, he ran for a position on the board anyway.

A few days before the election, in an effort to influence the election results in favor of the misguided boyfriend, a person (or persons) unknown committed an act of forgery by concocting a phony document and mailing it to all association members. Using computer technology, they cut and pasted the signatures of the board members who had signed the previously mentioned letter, affixing them to a document stating that they had changed their minds and recanted. The fake document stated that they now supported the boyfriend's bid for election. The one missing signature on the forged letter was that of the boyfriend's board-member girlfriend, who had not signed the initial letter from the board to association members.

A few days before the election, a person (or persons) unknown committed an act of forgery by concocting a phony document and mailing it to all association members.

Though this amateurish attempt to influence the board election failed, the forgery victims (six board members and the entire association) were extremely upset. At the annual association meeting, association members demanded that the board conduct an investigation of the forgery. The board decided that such an investigation was necessary to restore the integrity of the six board members and the association at large.

The forgery was committed on association letterhead stationery through computerized manipulation. The forged document was distributed through the intrastate and interstate postal system. So the forgery also entailed postal fraud. It was mailed to all unit owners with the intent to deceive them. If this situation was not exposed and corrected, all future correspondence from the association's executive board would be suspect. "I got a letter from the board—is it real?"

For more than a year after the incident, the board conducted an exhaustive investigation. It was done professionally and involved the local police, a private investigator, a forensics lab, and the association attorney. But during the time the board conducted its investigation, it was harassed (by suspects and/or accomplices) through anonymous websites, mailings, and other assorted pranks. The harassment was intended to mock, deflect suspicion, and scare board members. The tactics succeeded on one board member, who resigned near the end of the investigation ordeal.

At one point during the investigation, the boyfriend candidate was caught on a retail store security surveillance camera, buying merchandise for an insulting prank that was directed against the board president and his spouse. Not knowing he had been caught on videotape, the boyfriend denied his guilt several times when interrogated by the private investigator. Only when he was confronted with the videotape evidence of his purchase, did he admit guilt. His girlfriend (the board member) completely refused to cooperate with the board and the private investigator. All but one of those suspected of involvement in the forgery scheme refused to take association funded polygraphs.

From the crime's inception, the executive board had a short list of persons of interest. Proving the crime in a court trial, however, would be another thing—especially when you considered the expense to be incurred by the association. Until the case was filed, the association would incur about $15,000 of investigation expenses. Without divulging the details of the investigation to the association's membership, the board gave updates that included the costs incurred to date. At no time did the membership majority complain about the costs.

Until the case was filed, the association would incur about $15,000 of investigation expenses.

A couple of unit owners publicly stated that the whole investigation was a waste of the association's funds and the board's time. In the end, neither a civil nor criminal lawsuit was initiated against the forgery suspects. Instead, the board requested that the forger(s) privately confess to the current board of directors and apologize to the six board members who were victims of the forgery. In exchange for their confession, they would be offered anonymity for their actions (to be secured by the attorneys involved). They did not take the deal, but hinted at copping to a lesser plea—just not to the forgery itself. No guilt was ever legally established.

The Moral of the Story

My advice to condo owners, boards, and managers is that if a prospective board member is caught lying and cheating (whether on videotape or not), he or she should never be considered again for board membership. Such an ethical disqualifier should also be extended to the friends and facilitators of the liar.

The West Point Code of Honor states, "A cadet will not lie, cheat, steal or tolerate anyone who does." This is also my personal code of honor with the addendum that "the friends of my enemies are also my enemies."

Chapter 25

How Bad Can It Get?

In the twilight of my condo career, I was asked to consult for an association that was in danger of going bankrupt. After almost thirty years of condo experience, I had the confidence to take the engagement. The initial SOS call came out of the blue. At my first meeting with the association's board president, he outlined the association's status as he understood it at that time.

> *I told the association board that the association, bankrupt or not, could be bought out by an investor group and turned into an apartment building.*

After some initial "pre-game coaching" from me, the board president discovered within a couple months that his association was losing more than he or the other board members ever imagined. A book-length case study could be written about their dilemma, but I will only summarize here.

This association and community consisted of 140 condo units in one high-rise building on about four acres of property. The association's annual budget was about $500,000.

There was a five-member board and an on-and-off-site property manager. Mind you, he was not my idea of a community association manager. Some of the "lowlights" of the association's predicament were:

- ☐ It had a $500,000 loan at 9.5% interest from some faraway out-of-state bank.
- ☐ Condo fees were high.
- ☐ The monthly assessment delinquency rate was above ten percent.
- ☐ It owed a local law firm a large amount in delinquent assessment collection fees.
- ☐ The building had never-ending plumbing problems.
- ☐ Capital reserve funds were insignificant.
- ☐ The rental unit percentage was too high (if you can't sell it, rent it).
- ☐ There were abandoned units.
- ☐ The manager was overbilling for his services and materials.
- ☐ The board had condo-paralysis.
- ☐ Some units were being offered for sale for thirty-five cents on the dollar.

I told the association board that the association, bankrupt or not, could be bought out by an investor group and turned into an apartment building. That got their attention. Combining my experience with my CPA investigative skills, I suggested the following actions.

Short Term Actions

- ☐ Fire the property manager and/or take him to court.
- ☐ Self manage for three years if possible.
- ☐ Meet with the delinquent collections law firm and settle the debt for cents on the dollar.
- ☐ Have face-to-face meetings with delinquent members to find out why they're in arrears.
- ☐ Get a couple new board members at the upcoming election.

- Get some good volunteers.
- Review every budget line item for legitimacy and possible savings.
- File civil liens for collection of delinquent assessments and acceleration.
- Hire an experienced condo bookkeeper.

Long Term Actions

- Restructure large loan with a local bank at a lower rate of interest.
- Continue to self manage as long as possible.
- Amend bylaws with a rental percentage limitation clause.
- Build capital reserve.
- Look for a legitimate association manager or consult with someone like me. (I didn't want the manager job because it was too scary and too time consuming.)

Progress Report

A few years later, this association is still in existence. The board accomplished most of my recommendations. Their chances of survival have greatly improved, but there is still no room for error. How could it have gotten so bad? The three key ingredients for a condo disaster are:

- An unscrupulous property manager
- A naïve and/or a dysfunctional board
- Association membership apathy

Prey and a predator, that's all it takes...

Chapter 26

INDUSTRY ADVOCACY

Community Associations Institute

The Community Associations Institute (CAI) is referred to as "America's Advocate for Responsible Communities." It is a national organization that, through its resources, tries to help all types of homeowner associations (HOAs) to govern their communities in a competent manner.

Its resources include:

- ☐ Coursework
- ☐ Seminars
- ☐ Website
- ☐ Trade show expos
- ☐ *Common Ground* magazine
- ☐ Online library
- ☐ Professional certifications
- ☐ Networking
- ☐ Gold Star Community recognition

Generally speaking, HOAs that subscribe to CAI membership enable more competent management of member communities. I was a member of the organization for about ten years. Though no longer a member, I have always endorsed and continue to endorse CAI. I routinely pressure any condo associations under my influence to join this organization.

CAI can provide association boards and managers with all of the technical information and theory necessary to survive in the condo industry. The keyword here is "survive." Surviving can mean just getting by. Technical information and theory will enable reasonable success. Practical application is more difficult because the unexpected comes into play.

You see, community association management has two main aspects: property management and people management. The first requires technical skills. The second requires just the right mix of intangibles. The people management aspect is where most association boards and managers fail or end up in court. Even if CAI wanted to teach people management skills, I'm not sure it would be effective. Like so many other professions, you either have it or you don't.

There is no doubt that boards and managers have to deal with all types of personalities. Artsy, left-brained types are not well suited for the structure and rigidity of the condo environment. Pragmatic right-brained types usually do better. Nonetheless, a manager has to try to satisfy both extremes and everything in between. It takes an experienced perspective and a broad psychological skill set to achieve longevity in the industry.

As valuable a resource as CAI might be, an objective analysis of its raison d'être should take into consideration the following:

- ☐ It collects dues.
- ☐ It has trade and professional sponsors.
- ☐ It can foster dependency (intentional or unintentional).
- ☐ It could be subject to networking conflict of interest.
- ☐ It can create a false sense of security (accomplishment) to unsuspecting managers or boards.
- ☐ Its professional certification requirements should be more stringent (more education and experience).

The CAI organization has served its industry well since its inception. However, I believe the time has come for CAI to expand its influence and become more thorough with its services. The necessary infrastructure is in place.

Chapter 27

FUTURE TRENDS
MY CRYSTAL BALL

Modern condo history in the United States began in the 1950s and 1960s. At that time, the first baby-boomers were approaching adulthood. Now those baby-boomers are retiring, selling big homes, and buying condos. They will do so for the next fifteen to twenty-five years.

From the 1950s to the 1970s and into the early 1980s, the condo industry grew from infancy to adolescence. At the beginning, everything was new, and problems were few. As the baby boomers matured, the condo industry grew rapidly, and condo prices soared. From the late 1980s to the 2008 real estate crash, condo owners

> *There will be a great demand for qualified condo board members and condo association managers.*

began to understand the condo industry problems and dealt with them on a case-by-case basis. Until 2008, demand outstripped supply. Of course, that demand was fueled by the availability of easy credit (i.e., ninja mortgages, an acronym for: no income, no job, or assets).

Looking Ahead

Presently, condo values are showing signs of recovery. The industry is still growing and will grow rapidly as the boomers live out the last third of their lives. These condo boomers are not the easy-going, fall-in-line, retiree demographic of the past two generations. This Woodstock generation demographic is only beginning to test the viability of the present condo industry. The next twenty years will bring great challenges. So condo association managers, board members, and attorneys will need to be at the top of their game. In order to do that, the number and quality of industry leaders has to improve.

Supply and Demand

Early on in my financial consulting career (building investment portfolios), I was given some great advice by one of my firm's wholesalers from New York City. He had come to my local retail branch to push an investment product to our retail staff. During the course of his presentation, he said, "If you want to make money in the stock market, all you have to do is to learn how to surf the baby boomer wave. There were eighty million baby boomers born between 1945 and 1964. Whatever they're buying, the companies that are selling it are going to make a lot of money. Find those companies and invest in them."

Think about it. It has happened and will continue to happen until the boomers meet their ultimate demise. As the baby boomers graduated from colleges and entered the workforce, the demand for certain products drastically increased. It was just a factor of scale. Auto sales took off as they were buying their first cars. If you were invested in the auto industry companies, you did extremely well. Then came first home purchases. Had you invested in the home building industry, you would have made a fortune.

Then the boomers, as empty nesters, entered their peak earning years, and began to invest in stocks and bonds. The stock market soared to record highs. Investments in the financial industry (Wall Street) built fortunes. Think of the money made by securities underwriters with the initial public offerings (IPOs) of all the Internet companies.

What will be the living and lifestyle demands of the baby boomers over the next thirty years? Many advisors are saying that the boomers will sell their big homes and move into apartment and homeowner association communities (condos). Perhaps at the back half of those thirty years it will be retirement communities and nursing homes. Invest in these themes and trends, and you will make money.

But what about the future growth of condo communities? One thing is for sure. There are going to be a lot more condo communities coming online. Translation: there's going to be a great demand for qualified condo board members and condo association managers. Not only is there going to be demand for more of these people, but the condo industry is going to demand greater professionalism of industry talent.

Chapter 28

WORDS TO LIVE BY

I have had a wonderful life to date. Fortunate to be born healthy, I continue to take advantage of that good fortune by focusing on staying healthy and strong. My dad always preached that without good health, it's hard to be happy. He was crippled early in life from a bad fall, so I took his perspective on health seriously.

Investing my time in someone or something has always brought more fulfillment than an investment of money could have brought.

My fitness enabled me to work hard for my family, my parents, and the condo communities that I managed. It took a lot of energy to take care of my aging parents (for many years) while, at the same time, developing two daughters into scholar athletes. But investing my time in someone or something has always brought more fulfillment than an investment of money could have brought.

Without my father's philosophy, I never could have helped my daughters to, and through, the United States Military Academy at West Point. Without that early training, I could not have helped all of my condo communities attain CAI Gold Star ratings. I only wish my parents were alive to see the fruits of their labor, wisdom, and sacrifice.

H. Jackson Brown, Jr., wrote *Life's Little Instruction Book* to provide his son with wisdom he could refer to as he lived his life. In that same spirit, CAI leaders throughout the years have shared their advice and pearls of wisdom for better community association life. Here, then, are just a few of their tips to guide you and enhance your life and your community.

Be a Good Homeowner

- ☐ Review the covenants, conditions, restrictions, and other association documents before you buy a home.
- ☐ Read them again when you move in.
- ☐ Pay your assessments—on time.
- ☐ Attend the annual election meeting and vote.
- ☐ Read the newsletter.
- ☐ Follow the rules.
- ☐ Serve on the board or, at a minimum, attend the open board meetings.
- ☐ Volunteer to serve your community.
- ☐ Remember that you are a member of the community association. What is good for the association is good for you.

Be a Good Neighbor

- ☐ Keep televisions and music at reasonable volumes.
- ☐ Curb thy dog.
- ☐ Respect handicap parking spaces.
- ☐ Take care of your property.
- ☐ Share a smile with a neighbor.
- ☐ Offer to lend a hand.
- ☐ Welcome new neighbors into the community.
- ☐ Talk about problems. Direct conversation is more effective than sending a letter or banging on a wall.

Be a Good Board Member

- ☐ Serve because you care about your neighborhood, not because you have a hidden agenda.
- ☐ Communicate, communicate, and communicate some more.
- ☐ Make decisions with the common good in mind, not self-interest.
- ☐ Educate residents.
- ☐ Anticipate and prevent conflicts.
- ☐ Remember your fiduciary duty to protect, preserve, and enhance the value of the property.

Work with Difficult Personalities

- ☐ Be diplomatic.
- ☐ Listen.
- ☐ Remain calm.
- ☐ Remember, constructive criticism provides impetus to positive change.
- ☐ Work together—two people cooperating are more effective than one person telling another to change.

Stay Out of Debt

In addition to encouraging me to stay healthy, my dad also warned me to stay out of debt. He said that debt was the worst four-letter word. Whereas other common four-letter words are simply expressions of frustration or descriptions of bodily functions, debt is a terrible condition. It imprisons you to lenders and ultimately to your employer. It usually compromises your independence and principles. Time spent on repaying debt is time lost to family, friends, responsibilities, and activities.

Debt becomes evil when fueled by ostentation and greed.

When debt is incurred, few people know how to manage it wisely and to their advantage. Debt becomes evil when fueled by ostentation and greed. Only one of my condo associations incurred debt in its history. That association borrowed $60,000 to initiate a roof replacement program. It was a five-year loan that was paid back in two and a half years.

Banks should only lend money with realistic assurance that they will be repaid. Individuals can't demand financial discipline from their bankers and governments if they don't practice discipline themselves. If everyone stayed out of debt or knew how to handle it, life in the United States would be unrecognizable. But it would be better—more honest, principled, and real.

Respect Your Elders

The condo associations that I managed or consulted for during my thirty years in the industry were populated by an older demographic. Working with "old" is an art, whether

It takes wisdom to recognize and appreciate wisdom.

it's an old person or an old thing. It requires wisdom, patience, and sometimes a little intimidation.

When I was eighteen years young, my dad was sixty-two years old (that's why I called him "Pop"). I remember one early Saturday morning when our residence septic system pipe was clogged. The pipe had to be excavated by hand with a shovel and repaired under Pop's supervision. Pop was far from lazy, but he performed physical labor all week, and Saturday was a chance for him to rest and teach. While he sat in his chair directing me, I dug where he thought the pipe was located.

On that sweltering Saturday in 1968, I spent three hours finding the broken pipe, which was about two feet underground. Pop's memory of the pipe's location changed several times. After I located it, I had to unearth the entire length of pipe to find the break or clog. As I inhaled the perfumed air, I silently cursed at Pop, even though I was learning about sewer systems, digging efficiently, and life in general. By noontime, I completed the job despite the ninety-degree temperature. Pop and I reconciled without a word spoken, realizing that both of us accomplished a task that neither of us wanted to do.

Recently, my office and building front porch were remodeled and repaired by Ken from Ken's Carpentry. Working with a 200-year-old building is like working with a 90-year-old human. Even though it was difficult, Ken made it look easy. I observed his work and helped him a little. It reminded me of the days when I worked with Pop. Many times during the construction I found myself saying, "I wouldn't have thought of that," or "Why does he want me to do it this way?"

Now I'm past the age Pop was when I silently cursed at him on that steamy Saturday morning almost forty-eight years ago. The lessons learned from working with old people and old things can be extremely difficult but equally rewarding. Therein lies the conundrum. It takes wisdom to recognize and appreciate wisdom. Thanks, Pop. And thanks, Ken.

Live a Full Life

Older people do more reminiscing than younger people because they have more of the past and less of the future to think about. I think a lot about the past, now. Twenty-six years ago I had my first daughter—now serving as a first lieutenant in the U.S. Army. That was also the time I was approached by a group of condo activists to orchestrate a condo board coup. It was also the time I began a professional career as a financial consultant for Shearson Lehman Brothers. These three life-changing events occurred in a brief period in 1989 and brought a world of happiness and a sense of accomplishment to my life.

Every year since 1989 has been filled with excitement. My second daughter, born in 1991 and also a graduate of West Point, is serving her country as an Army lieutenant. All those years of raising two scholar athletes interspersed with years in the condo industry have provided me a life of great satisfaction.

Despite unexpected disappointment from time to time, my years in the condo management industry have been amazing. I hope you also find joy and satisfaction in your personal life and in your own condo endeavors.

Appendix A

PROPOSED CURRICULUM FOR COMMUNITY MANAGEMENT

As we head into the future, we need to have better education and experience requirements to enter the industry of community association management. The psychological profiles of successful association managers must also be assessed. In other words, what personality traits lend themselves to a successful career in condo association management? Professionalism is needed right now. The industry is behind the curve and eventually will demand better.

Perhaps CAI could establish a CAI University. Better yet, how about partnering with local regional vo-tech high schools? A homeowner association management program could also be offered in community colleges or technical institutes.

At a minimum, the goal of an HOA curriculum would be a two-year program (no summer recess) that gains enrollees an associate's degree in HOA management. Summers would be spent doing case studies or apprenticing with management company sponsors. Upon successful graduation, there would be a one-year experience requirement to earn a certification as a professional HOA manager.

Such a program would be more stringent than current CAI professional certification standards. The two-year degree program would have to cover the following aspects of HOA management.

Proposed Curriculum for Condo Management

Course: HOA Governance
I. Management styles
II. Board of Director's Responsibilities
III. HOA Documents
IV. Declaration
    A. Bylaws
    B. Amendments
V. Unit Owner's Manual
VI. State HOA laws
VII. ADA standards
VIII.Civil Rights

Course: HOA Financial Management
I. Elementary Accounting
II. Budgeting
III. HOA Financial Statements
IV. Operating Funds
    A. Capital Reserve Funds
    B. Audits
V. Basic Investing

Course: Facilities Management
I. Clubhouse
II. Pool
III. Athletic/Sports
IV. Other Recreational
V. Maintenance Building

Course: Building Construction
   I.   Basic Construction Terminology
   II. Construction Supervision
   III. Building Trades
        A. Carpentry
        B. Plumbing
        C. Electrical
        D. HVAC
        E. Roofing
        F. Siding
        G. Masonry
        H. Insulation
        I. Drywall
        J. Painting
        K. Flooring

Course: Insurance and Risk Management
   I.   Types of Insurance
        A. Property
        B. Liability
        C. Directors and Officers
        D. Auto
        E. Fidelity Bonds
        F. Worker's Compensation
        G. Umbrella Liability
        H. Other
   II. Risk Control
   III. Risk Prevention

Course: Landscape Management
   I.   Lawn Care and Mowing
   II. Tree Management
   III. Shrubbery Care and Management
   IV. Drainage

Course: Public Relations
   I.   Leadership
   II. Public Speaking

    III. Committee Organization

Course: Communications
    I.   Newsletter Publication
    II.   Internet Related
    III. Face to Face

Course: HOA Elections

Course: Storm Management

Course: Wildlife and Pest Control
    I.   Domestic vs. Feral
    II.   Insects
    III. Rodents
    IV. Waterfowl
    V.   Other

Course: HOA Case Studies

Course: Conflict Resolution
    I.   Role of the HOA Attorney
    II.   Confrontation Strategies
    III. Conflict Resolution

Practicum: One-Year Apprenticeship

Certainly, a prospective association manager who completes these courses over a two-year period is going to be a more qualified professional than the average manager in today's condo industry. There are some very qualified managers out there but they are an extreme minority. Ultimately, the demand for better managers will bring change and improvement.

Appendix B

GLENCREEK

A CASE STUDY ~ APRIL 2011

Glencreek began its existence as an apartment complex. Originally developed in the early 1970's, the complex was a great place for young people. According to the people who lived there at the time, Glencreek was a magnet for young singles, who described it as "party city—a happening place to live."

The Early Years

On November 30, 1981, the developer issued a public offering statement that began the process of converting Glencreek from an apartment complex to a condominium. It became the first condominium conversion in Lancaster County, Pennsylvania. Tenants who may not have had a care in the world—except what to wear to the next pool party—were suddenly faced with the need to think about new housing options, moving to a different apartment complex, or buying the unit they lived in.

A news report in the local newspaper on October 29, 1981, said about 300 tenants came to a meeting during which they were told their apartments would soon be available for sale. Prices would vary, depending on size and view. The average "as is" price was $47,815. We do not know the number of tenants who actually purchased and continued to live in their units, but we do know that many investors purchased units to rent to others. And of course, new owners who had never lived at Glencreek also purchased here. Thus began a new life for this community as Glencreek Condominium.

Fiscal year 1982–1983 was Year 1 for the new Glencreek Condominium Association and its newly formed executive board. Everything was new to them. Everything had to be learned. From landscaping to pool maintenance to clubhouse maintenance to unit repairs to capital investments, a brand new and very steep learning curve presented itself. This fledging executive board began its work using the starting points created by Prudential. Not only did the board have no prior experience, it had no prior history of other condominium conversions from which to learn.

The first monthly assessments, ranging from $80 to $153, were established by Prudential based on whatever information they wanted to share. There was no way to really know if those numbers were right or wrong. Compared to 2011 assessments, however, it would appear that these assessments were more than adequate for 1982.

Quite a bit has been written—and much has been said—about the poor results achieved by the executive boards of those early years. I believe it unfair to make too much of their record. Well-meaning, inexperienced unit owners stepped up and volunteered to serve on the board. I believe they did the best they could with the challenges they faced.

Nevertheless, by 1990 Glencreek was in trouble. Capital reserves were virtually nonexistent, budgets were increasing yearly, special assessments were the order of the day, and necessary maintenance and capital expenditures were behind schedule. There was considerable unrest in the community, and the executive board was losing support from the community.

In the spring of 1990, a new budget was proposed for fiscal year 1990–1991, but was soundly defeated by the members of the association. It called for operating expenses of $860,256 to be paid for with income from assessments and other miscellaneous sources of $797,996. The shortfall of $62,260 would be covered by cashing two association CDs. Had it been approved, the budget would have increased monthly assessments by nineteen percent.

In addition to defeating this budget, the owners elected a new executive board that developed a new budget, implemented an audit by a new accounting firm, and began the arduous task of rebuilding both the physical and financial infrastructure of Glencreek.

Consider the following facts: From April 1990 to April 2010, total inflation was 69.1 percent (according to Inflation-Data.com). If the proposed 1990–1991 budget of $860,256 had been allowed to grow at the same inflation rate until now, the budget in 2010 would have been $1,454,951. I don't even want to contemplate what the monthly assessments would be now, but the community was blessed with a very different outcome—the result of careful, conservative administration of the resources entrusted to the new executive board.

Each year, on the back page of the annual budget, the executive board shows the complete history of capital improvement expenditures since 1982. This is made available so each unit owner can calculate the cumulative adjusted cost basis of his/her condo unit. This history also reflects the enormous progress made since 1990. Some say that's when the Renaissance began.

The Renaissance

The executive board elected in April 1990 had a mandate from the community: cut costs, conserve money whenever possible, and maintain Glencreek properties. Implicit in this mandate was the requirement to build reserves while keeping assessments as low as possible. These are complementary, but conflicting goals—a daunting task to say the least. For a while, the board met at least weekly, often into the wee hours. Priorities were the budget, critical maintenance, and landscaping, but everything was reviewed: computer services, accounting fees, consulting fees, office supplies, salaries, and in-house maintenance. All were scrutinized. In addition, a major audit was ordered.

A new management structure began to form and, while the basic modus operandi was "emergency," a new calm began to emerge. Gradually, the new hands at the helm began to steer a more sensible course.

The new budgetary controls and more effective cost management—while critical to Glencreek's future—did not magically result in adequate cash reserves. But significant cuts to fiscal year 1991 operating expenses allowed the board to reduce monthly assessments by forty-three percent, offset by a special assessment of $60,000 for roof replacements (an average of $160 per unit).

These two actions restored monthly assessments to a more realistic level and initiated a more aggressive approach to critical capital replacements. It may not have yet been obvious, but the overall financial health of the community was already improving.

Not everyone was in favor of the budget cuts. While the majority of unit owners strongly supported the board's decisions, some were fearful the cuts would undermine the bucolic environment at Glencreek. Some correspondence received by the board rhapsodized about Glencreek's rolling lawns, beautiful trees, and spacious, well-maintained landscapes. Some expressed fears that amenities such as the pool, tennis courts, clubhouse, and social activities would be degraded. These reactions were normal. After all, no one wants a lowered level of service. It is always a problem of competing priorities and limited resources.

Here is the reality: as unit owners, we are both the recipients and the providers of services and amenities. Through our monthly assessments, we each provide to the entire community the resources necessary for maintenance and improvement. And, of course, corrections are always needed.

The overriding mission of the executive board should always be one of balance. After all, the board is nothing more than a function of the community. The board must administer the cash inflows and outflows to best serve the long-term interests of the community. It must balance immediate needs against long-term needs, current operating costs against saving for the future.

The following bar chart graphically portrays the Board's track record:

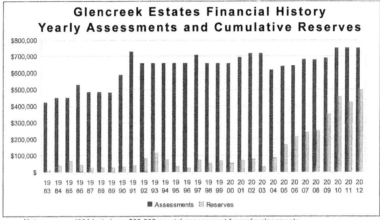

	Glencreek Estates Financial History Yearly Assessments and Cumulative Reserves

Notes: 1991 includes a $60,000 special assessment for roof replacements
1992-2000 – Board President's Pledge: No common assessment increases
1997 - includes a $50,044 special assessment for over-budget snow removal costs
2003 – Leo Rosenberger became Association Manager
2004 – Sewer costs ($121,000) removed from common assessments
2011 – Accelerated spending on capital projects
2012 – Next Year's Budget

As shown in the notes above, special assessments are included in assessments. This explains some of the year-to-year distortions. Also, please note that sewer costs were separated from assessments in 2004. Finally, the 2011 dip in reserves comes from our acceleration of capital projects during a period when interest rates were low.

Doing the research for this little history reminded me of some facts. I remembered that the board president in 1991 had pledged no new common assessment increases. That pledge remained in place for eight years. While unit owners must have welcomed this pledge—given the history of regular and excessive increases—it limited the executive board's ability to build necessary capital reserves. This unintended consequence is clear from the chart.

What emerges out of a study of this chart are three essential phases: Phase 1 (from 1983 through 1990) I will call the Beginner Phase, notable for rapidly rising assessments, ineffective cost control and no increase in capital reserves. Phase 2 (from 1991 through 2003) I will call the Control Phase, during which assessments were essentially level and capital projects were much better managed, but reserves continued to lag. Phase 3 is the Growth Phase.

The Growth Phase, 2004 to Present

Assessments increased at more sensible rates and capital reserves grew steadily. I believe we are now headed into what I will call the Mature Phase. Glencreek has come very close to achieving that balance I mentioned earlier. It is moving into a period of optimizing (or fine tuning) the mix of operations, maintenance, landscaping, capital replacements and improvements, as well as the enhancement of physical amenities—the clubhouse, pool, tennis courts, maintenance barn, etc.

A Final Word about Glencreek

The history of Glencreek's financial life is also a history of the decisions and actions taken by many executive boards. Those boards were populated by dedicated unit owners who volunteered their time, skills, knowledge, work, and devotion to the entire community. I believe each one did his or her best to improve the quality of life at Glencreek. Mistakes were made, but lessons were learned, and learned well. In the end, Glencreek is on course.

I know we will face uncertain times. The economy threatens us on all sides. Housing values will probably be slow to recover, but I believe the future of Glencreek Condominium Association will be a happy one. Together, we can handle whatever comes our way.

Appendix C

Letter from the Auditor's Auditor

Joseph Smith, CPA
100 Stone Road
Lancaster, PA 17601

August 4, 2010
Glencreek Condominium Association
ATTN: Leo Rosenberger, Community Association Manager
One Water Drive
Honesdale, PA 17173

Dear Mr. Rosenberger:

In accordance with our engagement letter of February 2, 2010, I have analyzed the financial records of Glencreek Condominium Association as of June 30, 2010 and for the three-month period then ended. I did not perform an audit of the Association's financial statements for the purpose of conforming to generally accepted accounting principles.

Agreed-Upon Procedures:
1. Review the bank statement and check images for payees, amounts and signature. Trace for unusual payees. Compare signatures for reasonableness. Review checks of large amounts.

2. Select a sample of checks recorded in the Operating Account and trace them to invoices.
3. Select a sample of vendor files and trace the invoice to the general ledger for proper classification.
4. Review the check sequence in the Operating Account and inquire about skipped checks and voided checks.
5. Review the credit card statements for documentation of charges.
6. Review the bank reconciliations prepared by the accounting personnel, noting any unusual entries
7. Scan the general ledger for unusual fluctuation of income and expense accounts.

Conclusion:

In performing the above-referenced procedures, I found no issues of noncompliance or improper financial and accounting practices. The Association is using sound financial practices to record and report its financial activity.

Should you have any questions related to the issues raised in this letter, please contact me at your earliest convenience.

Sincerely,

Joseph Smith, CPA

CPSIA information can be obtained at www.ICGtesting.com
Printed in the USA
BVOW06s1544040316

439035BV00007B/5/P